Rules Don't Work for Me

Rules Don't Work for Me

My Code for Business and Life

Gail Summers

BUSINESS EXPERT PRESS
Leader in applied, concise business books

Rules Don't Work for Me: My Code for Business and Life

First published in 2021 by
Business Expert Press, LLC
222 East 46th Street, New York, NY 10017
www.businessexpertpress.com

ISBN-13: 978-1-94858-071-7 (paperback)
ISBN-13: 978-1-94858-072-4 (e-book)

Business Expert Press Business Career Development Collection

Collection ISSN: 2642-2123 (print)
Collection ISSN: 2642-2131 (electronic)

First edition: 2021

10 9 8 7 6 5 4 3 2 1

Description

It is tough to succeed in these days whether it's the business of life or the business of business. It can be especially tough for outliers. Here is the personal code for success for one outlier. Of course, it all depends on how one defines success. If success means happiness at home and in the workplace, this is the code for you.

In this book, we will explore nine principles to live and work by from an outlier perspective. This is not saying these principles and this personal code are the only way. They are just one way. The hope is that you will find your own way and embrace your own outlierness and uniqueness. The principles are: know thyself, develop courage, develop mastery, grow your pennies, be tenacious, have faith, lead the way, challenge the system, and save the world.

Along with these principles, I will share a little of my story and stories from my clients who came to me for career coaching. I have changed the names of clients to protect their confidentiality.

Perhaps you wonder. What is an outlier? There is no one perfect definition. It means you may think different than others or feel left out or you don't relate to the status quo, or the status quo makes no sense. It may mean that whenever you follow whatever rules are set for you that those same rules don't seem to work for you. My suggestion is to consider rethinking the rules or make your own rules. Here's mine.

Keywords

workplace happiness; job satisfaction; career coaching; courage; know thyself; business success; outlier; leadership

Contents

Acknowledgments

Thank you and much gratitude to the following people. They helped me, inspired me, and encouraged me.

- Suzanne Potts, developmental editor who helped me flush out my thoughts.
- Jeff Braucher, editor, who helped me get the manuscript ready.
- Kathy Schuit, artist, who drew all the great cartoons.
- All the millennials who helped me understand their perspective of the workplace.
- Most of all, to my clients, especially Jacob, from whom I learned so much.

Thank you to my husband and sweetie-pie, Ken. And my little dog, Sam.

A special thank you to you for reading this. Live well.

Introduction

Rules generally don't work for me. I often don't fit in. I feel like an outsider, someone who doesn't sit inside the normal bell curve. An outlier.

Outliers know what it feels like to live outside the norm, and I would venture to guess that plenty of people who seem to be living inside of what is commonly considered to be *the norm* feel different in some way. They can relate to the feeling that the so-called rules for living a good life don't apply to them. They likely sense they have something unique to offer the world, even if they have yet to discover a way to focus their energy. If you are an outlier, I hope my own outlier story and my model for thriving in business and life can assist you in following your unique path and developing your special gifts to share with us all.

In the course of my life, I've discovered that it's not always necessary to follow the rules. I'm not talking about laws or safety rules. I'm talking about the rules and expectations—best practices and expert advice—we buy into and apply to our personal and professional lives. The rules that set the societal standards for how we are to behave, communicate, interact, and appear. As an outlier, I have learned to create my own rules (or model or code) for living. Over time, I've discovered that *being* reflects my experiences and unique vision. Who am I to talk about unique vision and personal codes? I am nobody special, no billionaire, no famous entity. What do I have? I am happy. I have success according to my definition. I have the capacity to love and be loved. To date, I have no regrets. I didn't realize this was special until I became a career coach. The number one issue I hear with clients is, "I am unhappy." Thus, I offer you my perspective.

As outliers, we see the world from a different perspective and often pay a price for our unconventional responses to people and situations. We get fired. We experience loneliness, restlessness, alienation. An outlier, as defined by various dictionaries, is a person differing from all the members of a group, a person who is detached, isolated, less accessible, an aberration, an anomaly, somebody who can cause serious problems, who doesn't fit, or a person who is exceptional, special, even a genius. Our circumstances, experiences, heritage, ethnicity, nationality, language, community, home environment, family's values, gender, sexual preference, appearance, physical attributes, skills, gifts, talents, disabilities, personality, quirks, religion, beliefs, politics, and class all contribute to our sense of self. By fully embracing these aspects of ourselves that might be seen as different by others or by mainstream society, we can begin to explore how they can be best utilized in life and business.

***

I grew up in the backwoods of Alaska. We had no close neighbors, and school was an hour bus ride away. In winter, my two younger sisters and I often played outside when it was –20 degrees. Being the oldest, I felt it was my responsibility to protect all of us. My mom was always telling me to take care of my sisters. I kept a sharp eye out for moose or bears and stood ready to rescue my sisters if they happened to fall in the river or hurt themselves while we explored the woods.

You might be wondering what my parents were doing while my sisters and I were chasing away bears by banging on tin cans. My dad, who was in the Air Force, drove our only car to work every day, leaving us stranded in the backwoods until he came home late, and drunk. My mom was petite and totally dependent on my father. I was the only one of us girls to witness him hitting my mom. I would take pains to protect my sisters by distracting them so that they didn't see what was happening. I vowed to myself that when I got big enough and strong enough, I would protect my mom from my father.

My father was a big man, but I was taller than average, younger and faster, and most significant, sober. And, from spending so much time in the woods, I had developed the ability to evaluate any danger I was facing. If my father came home drunk and got violent, I could assess how drunk he was and what my chances were of getting my sisters and mom out of his way. One day, when I was 12 years old, he came home drunk and extra mean. My sisters and mom were in the back bedroom. He started to strike me. I grabbed a small cast iron frying pan and beat at him until he staggered against the wall and looked at me wide-eyed with his mouth hanging open. He never bothered any of us again.

Born of necessity, I developed skills that a kid my age would normally not need to develop. I learned to listen, observe, strategize, calculate, protect, defend, and stand up for myself and others who were less powerful. The unpleasant circumstances of my home life along with my natural physical and leadership abilities allowed me to develop skills that I've used in my various careers as well as in my approach to personal growth.

As a child, I was an avid reader and read all my dad's Air Force books, which, along with a set of encyclopedias, were sometimes the only books in the house. My dad worked in the preventive medicine division of the Air Force, so we had books on first aid, survival in the Arctic, and weightlifting. I practiced first aid on my stuffed animals. However, I knew it wasn't enough to learn first aid from books; I had to have real survival skills. I started following the weightlifting program used by the Air Force, and because I didn't have access to a gym or real weights, I lifted bricks. I also compiled an emergency day pack filled with *supplies* to survive in the woods in case we got stranded. Supplies consisted of matches, teabags, dried soups, flashlights, ponchos, a knife, chocolate, fishing line and hooks, bug spray, sunscreen, water, a compass, and a signal mirror. To this day, I carry a day pack like this.

The first time I knew I was different was when I was in seventh grade and my entire class was transferred to a large middle school on the Air Force base. Every teenager within a 100 miles was bussed to this school. I'd been an outstanding student in elementary school and got a lot of positive attention from my teachers for my straight A's and creative writing. I was outgoing and comfortable with my small group of friends. At the new bigger school, I became an outcast. I wasn't making new friends, and I had no idea what I was doing wrong. The boys didn't talk to me, and I'm sure, in retrospect, I intimidated them. I was tall and strong, and I didn't giggle or make small talk.

At my new school, a teacher asked me, seemingly out of nowhere, if my "wetback mom swam the river." My mom was Mexican. However, because my family lived in Alaska with no relatives nearby, I had no connection to this heritage. In fact, I don't recall my mom ever overtly acknowledging it. Perhaps the teacher deduced that my mom was Mexican because I was talking about how she made tacos for dinner. I really didn't understand what the teacher was saying, but I knew from her tone that it wasn't a good thing. She laughed, like she was making a cute joke. I punched her hard in the nose and got suspended for three days. I don't know what happened to her, but she never bothered me again. In fact, nobody bothered me after that, which only added to my feeling of being an outcast.

While I was in high school, my mom got approved to take in foster children. She stopped fostering after a little boy she returned to his biological mother was killed by her. It devastated me to see my mom's heart break. I decided in that moment that I would never have children of my own. I didn't want the responsibility or the potential heartbreak. I'd taken good care of my sisters and the foster children. I'd done my duty. I'd been a parent. My desire to go to college, to be independent and explore the world overrode any biological or emotional impulse I might have had to raise children. I have never regretted this decision, though it alone has made me an outlier among some of my women friends.

***

When I graduated high school, I chose to attend the University of Arizona in Tucson. It just so happened that I had lots of relatives from my mom's side in Tucson. Their food, festivals, and traditions were foreign to me, but they welcomed me and loved me. I was only the second member of the family to attend college and was treated as special. Every weekend, I bicycled to Nana and Tata's house. I helped Nana make giant, translucent Sonoran tortillas over an outdoor wood-fired grill. Nana did not speak English, and I did not speak Spanish, but we managed to communicate through gestures, food, and laughter.

Everything in my life was new. I was connecting with family I'd never known about before and learning about a cultural heritage I'd never been exposed to. I was living in a scorching hot desert landscape, navigating city life, and meeting new classmates. I hoped I would have better luck making friends than I'd had in high school. That was not to be. I found that I didn't know how to convey who I really was to my new classmates. When asked where I was from, I had to explain I was not an Eskimo. I got tired of it. Apparently, I also dressed funny and talked funny. I didn't fit in. So, as I'd done many times in the past, I applied myself to my studies and forgot about having a social life.

I was studying chemistry with plans to become a psychiatrist and save all the depressed housewives in the world (my mom). Then the alligator jaw appeared. The professor put a pin between the jaw bones. How much pressure was the pin exerting down on the jaw, how much pressure was the jaw exerting down, and how much pressure was the jawbone exerting up? Impossible! I struggled to maintain average grades in this class and finally realized I didn't have the grades or the passion to go on to medical school. I changed my major to creative writing, with a minor in journalism and graduated with an A average.

Not long after I graduated, I became engaged to a wonderful and wealthy man. He let me know that he wanted to buy me an expensive, somewhat flashy emerald ring. This evidence of his commitment jarred me into the realization that I didn't really love him. I sensed that we both represented something to the other that was missing, which we were pretending marriage would magically fix. He was a good man, but I couldn't in good conscience marry him.

***

"What do you have for a female college grad who wants to travel?" I asked the Army recruiter.

"Meet me for coffee and we'll see," the recruiter told me.

I belonged suddenly! I had a starched uniform, gold second lieutenant bars and the Military Police crossed pistols embroidered above my pocket. I was a good officer. I fit in. The Military Police and I shared a common value—the mandate to protect. Promotions came easily. Eventually I was stationed in Germany, a country I fell in love with. I was going to stay in the Army, become a *lifer*, and retire a colonel. It was perfect. But, the truth was that I was bored. After a few years, I requested a transfer to public affairs, where I could write for the Army newspaper. With a degree in creative writing and journalism, I felt this was a career track that might be more challenging and interesting for me. Request rejected.

One day, a female sergeant confided in me that a male lieutenant colonel was demanding sexual favors. If she didn't comply, he would ruin her career. She was scared. She was a single parent and an excellent sergeant. I was me, and I was a military police officer. I protected. I confronted the lieutenant colonel and threatened to expose him and destroy his career if he didn't stop harassing the female sergeant. He complied. I was lucky. It was an act of bravado on my part. He outranked me and could have negatively impacted my own career. For the first time, I thought about the meaning of courage. Nonetheless, I was still bored. It was time for me to move on.

With time, I moved on again and landed in the worst job I've ever held. I became part of a civilian contractor workforce that worked for a federal organization. Running oversight on us were more than 25 government employees, mostly ready to retire, trying to improve their portfolio, or assigned to the center as punishment. It was a bad fit. I did not belong there. My ideals and ethics were not the same. My passion for innovation and sense of time frames, format, and budget did not align with their agenda. The only good part was my staff. I hung in there for seven years, growing more and more restless and grumpy. One fateful day I was tasked with selecting a subcontractor. This contract was termed best value, not low bid. I was expected to select the management favorite. I did not. I selected best value and debate ensued. Argument followed.

After I was fired, I realized I finally had a feel for who I was and decided to go to coaching school. I was one of the few students paying my own way. Many of the other students came from big corporations and held important titles. I was unemployed, trying to reinvent myself. I followed the coaching model and guidelines set by the International Coaching Federation. I followed the established best practices. I emulated what successful coaches were doing: executive coaching for top leaders and highly motivated clients who worked for big companies that paid for the coaching. In short order, I realized I was not interested in C-suite clientele. I wanted to work with oddball innovators, tough cases, and outliers who, by the way, usually cannot afford coaching. Today, I am trying to find new ways to coach and creating my own coaching model for the outliers among us.

The call to write came to me as my stepdad lay dying. I started taking notes. How could I capture this experience in a story? In college, I was often admonished by professors for not writing in complete sentences. However, while sipping coffee at a café and eavesdropping on conversations, I had an epiphany that has informed my writing ever since. A particular conversation between two women at a nearby table was the source of this epiphany. I listened carefully to their dialogue, ripe with incomplete, run-on, overlong, and even one-word sentences. No grammar rules adhered to. Their dialogue portrayed emotion and a sense of rhythm reflected through vocal variety and pause. One lady asked the other lady, "What's your price point?"—code for "What can you afford?" *Price point* is nice, more polite, even though it is less specific. Real dialogue does not follow rules. I decided I wanted to write how people authentically speak.

I'm interested in how people think and feel. Do they think and feel in words? Images? Could I develop emotional realism by creating my own way to use language? Could I take real life, fictionalize it, and then make it feel real? Could I add a sense of lyricism to bring to life the music of life? My first novel is about my family, inspired by my stepdad's dying. It is not a runaway bestseller novel, but it sells consistently, and I get a small royalty check every month. Plus I won two awards. I am slowly mastering the craft of fiction my way.

I'm happy and I love my life. Happiness is part of my definition of success. I think I owe it to being on outlier, to making decisions that veered from the norm, to recognizing when I didn't fit in, to moving on. Right now, the coronavirus swirls around, and I wonder, if I were to lie dying of this awful disease, what I would regret. Not getting my PhD—even at my age. I did a little research and ended up enrolling in a doctoral program in industrial psychology.

For me, being an outlier as a kid was about not belonging, not fitting in, muddling along trying to meet others' expectations. I now realize that being an outlier propelled me on a journey to find myself and understand who I am, to know what I believe in and what I stand for. Being an outlier also gave me the courage to defend myself and my values. It's not so much about breaking the rules as it is about reinventing the rules.

This book explores and explains the personal code I attempt to live by. Here is my code; I offer it to you in hopes that it will inspire you to create your own code:

- Know thyself
- Develop courage
- Develop mastery
- Grow your pennies

- Cultivate tenacity
- Have faith
- Lead the way
- Challenge the system
- Save the world

Just remember that we wouldn't be who we are without the richness and diversity of our experience. We may need help to overcome the impact of trauma, we may need to grow some skills, but each one of us is unique and has something special and profound to contribute to the world.

CHAPTER 1

Know Thyself

This above all: to thine own self be true.

—**William Shakespeare,** *Hamlet*

To thine own self be true…. It implies that we know who we are, but what if we don't? What if we are just muddling through our lives? And what if our muddling has brought us success? What if we have a career, home, and family. But what if this life path is not what we want? What if we don't know what we want? Or who we are? To thine own self be true…. We can't do or be what we don't know.

Make it thy business to know thyself, which is the most difficult lesson in the world.

—Miguel de Cervantes

Know Thyself: What Does It Mean?

We think we know who we are. But, do we? Are we who other people think we are? Let's be honest. I think most folks don't. Who are you?

My client Dean knew one thing about himself: He was not good at marketing or selling. However, an assessment I conducted with him indicated he should be excellent at marketing. Dean was startled to learn this, but based on this new information, decided to experiment with different marketing methods. He learned that yes, he did indeed have an aptitude for marketing. As he honed his marketing skills, his business grew, and his professional relationships improved.

Know Thyself: Why?

Observe all men; thy self most.

—Benjamin Franklin

To learn about yourself gives you power. In fact, it's a superpower to truly know yourself. If we can learn about ourselves and truly know ourselves, we can accomplish anything discussed in this book. If we don't, we will muddle.

Knowing ourselves gives us decision-making power, which gives us the ability to shape our destiny. It gives us communication power, which can strengthen our impact and deepen our relationships. It gives us job-hunting power, which gives us a better chance to find a job or career that is a good fit. It gives us leadership power. It gives us courage, which allows us to face fear, stand up for others, and resist social pressure. It gives us power to know and manage our biases, which puts us in a better position to reach out to the world. To know ourselves gives us power to choose how we live life.

Millennial podcaster Megan Tan made the decision to turn down a job offer with a national magazine in favor of beginning her podcast-audio career in a closet. She feared if she took the magazine job, she might get sidetracked and fall off the career path she wanted for herself. She is now an audio producer in New York City. Her podcasts from her days in the closet are superb and give insight to millennialness. I've listened to every one of them.

Know Your Values

There are three things extremely hard: steel, a diamond, and to know one's self.

—Benjamin Franklin, 1750, ***Poor Richard's Almanack***

Begin the quest to learn about yourself by exploring your values. What is a value? A value is "a principle that gives meaning to our lives and allows us to persevere through adversity," write psychologists Barb Markway and Celia Ampel in *The Self-Confidence Workbook*. Values act as our personal code of conduct. Many of us don't know our values. We lean on the values of our parents, church, or society in general. How do we identify our own values?

Make a List

Keep it simple. Make a list. It is surprising how much a list can tell us. What we include. What we don't include.

Make a list of people. Who is important to you and why? For example, you may identify your family or your boss as important. Explore why they are important. One may represent love, and the other may represent livelihood. Perhaps you include your neighbor on the list. Why? Perhaps your neighbor represents community. What emerges? Think about this: Make a list of people who are offensive to you. What does that say about who or what you value?

Make a list of character traits. Write down character traits you admire. Identify the traits quickly, without thinking too much. Stuck?

Try watching movies. Observe the characters. What do they do? What do you admire about them? What about them makes you angry? I cannot watch Westerns where buffalo are killed for sport. I get angry. One of my values is to be kind to animals, to be respectful of wildlife. Movies I like for observing character traits include:

- *Hunt for Red October:* Watch Captain Ramius.
- *Batman: The Dark Knight:* Observe Alfred.
- *Ip Man 2:* Observe Ip in action as well as nonaction.
- *Hidden Figures:* Keep an eye on Dorothy.
- *Key Largo:* Observe all three main characters, especially the decisions they make.

Make a list of things you want to do. Perhaps it's the famous bucket list that identifies all the things you want to do in your life. Perhaps it's a wish list that identifies your dreams for the future. Perhaps it's the glorious when-I-win-the-lottery list. What shows up in these lists?

My bucket list looks like this:

- Learn to scuba dive—done
- Go to Mongolia
- Create a giant garden—done
- Finish my PhD—started
- Write a novel—done

Consider a visual list. Do this by making a vision board or collage or some visual representation of the people, things, or accomplishments you admire or hope to attain. What does it look like?

Make an elimination list. Identify everything you'd like to delete, avoid, or minimize in your life. Perhaps expand your list to the world. What would you like to eliminate? After you eliminate, what is left?

Make a happiness list. Identify all the times you were happy in your life. Why were you happy? Was it pure wonderful play? Was it pride of accomplishment? Was it giving or being loved? What emerges? Or, do the opposite. Make an unhappiness list. Identify all the times you were unhappy. What triggered your unhappiness? Do you see any patterns?

Analyze a Meaningful Event

Think about your life. What are the most meaningful events? Think about one striking event that made an impact on you. What happened?

My friend and client, Galin, came to me ready to fight for any cause presented to her. Sometimes she did this without getting all the information or without thinking. She simply took on the fight, usually for the perceived underdog. I asked her to tell me about a significant event in her past. She remembered a day when she was young. The other kids teased and picked on her relentlessly. One bully boy pulled her hair so hard that Galin screeched and swung around to swat him. The teacher saw her strike the boy and punished her for causing trouble. Galin was furious but not allowed to speak in her own defense. The bully said nothing. The other kids cowered along the sidelines and said nothing. The more Galin objected, the more the teacher reprimanded her. Today, she works as a legal advocate for a nonprofit that protects abused moms and children. After analyzing the hair-pulling event, Galin came to see why her most important value today is to protect herself and fight against unfairness. This new insight is helping her to move forward and reshape her future. She is learning how to pick her fights, how to advocate more effectively for victims' rights, and when to let go of some fights.

Align Your Values to Your Behavior

Does our behavior reflect our values? Does our behavior reflect an ugly side of our values? Clyde seemed like a calm, peaceful man. He told me he was interested in religion, and that his number one value was spirituality. But, that value only pertained to his form of spirituality. He openly despised concepts of spirituality and faith that differed from his. He claimed they were evil. Colleagues said Clyde was *righteous* and *pushy*. He told me he felt it was his calling to eradicate evil and spread the news about his own brand of spirituality. He requested coaching on how to do this more effectively. I declined him as a client.

Linda said courage was her number one value, yet she refused to do anything she feared. Linda's performance appraisal noted that she needed to develop *backbone* and learn how to manage risk. Linda has been my client for two years now. She has worked hard on growing and developing her capacity to face fear. And, guess what? She wants to start her own small business.

Both Clyde and Linda were unaware of how their values were not aligned. Clyde's behavior reflected that he was a bigot, not a spiritual man. At first, Linda's behavior reflected that she was a coward, not a courageous person. Perhaps Clyde admired spirituality, and Linda admired courage, but neither behaved accordingly. When we think of our values, we must also consider how we behave. Does our behavior reflect what we value?

Review: Know Yourself and Your Values

Tools	Things to think about
Make a list	Create a list. Consider one of the following: • People you like/people you don't like • Character traits that you admire/that make you angry • Things you want to do list/eliminate • Things that make you happy/unhappy • Create a visual list of any of the above
Analyze a meaningful event	Describe a meaningful event in your life How has this event impacted your life?
Align your values to your behavior	Go back to your values and reidentify them How does your behavior reflect those values?

Know What Motivates You

Find out who you are and do it on purpose.

—Dolly Parton

Motivation is something that causes us to behave in a certain way. It is our willingness to do something. Or, our unwillingness to do something. Motivation is why we do things. How do we find out what motivates us?

Look for Evidence

Consider examining the past for evidence or clues. Think about the things in the past you worked hard for. Was it saving money, getting good grades in school, buying a car or a house? Was it learning and mastering a skill or sport? Was it building or creating something? Was it in service of a cause?

Then, look closer. What was it specifically that motivated you to work hard? Was it something tangible, such as a paycheck or a reward? Was it something intangible, such as the approval of others? Was it something internal, such as feeling good about yourself, knowing you did a good job? Was it something you needed to survive or protect yourself?

Look for the smoking gun, the answer hidden in plain sight. Ask yourself: What would make me stay seven years in this dull job? What is making me stay in this career field? What got me to work so hard on that project?

Define Success

When I first met Selina, she said she felt something was missing. She was a successful lawyer: big paycheck, nice house and car, beautiful clothes, a personal trainer, and season tickets to the opera. I asked her to describe what success meant for her. She was enjoying all the perks of her job, at least superficially. But, with time, she realized she was living according to other people's definition of success, mainly her parents. She realized that for her, success meant to make a difference in the world. She wanted to save the world (a common theme among my clients). She is now a *water lawyer* who fights to protect the underground rivers in the Southwest.

How we define success can motivate us if we are honest about what success means to us. There are things we all need, such as safety, security, food, health. But, what makes us happy as individuals? What makes us *feel successful?* What makes us feel we live a good life? The answers to these questions may surprise us. It certainly surprised me. I am a college-educated, modern professional woman, yet part of my definition of success is to be a good wife. Sounds old-fashioned. I suppose it depends on how you define *wife*. Other parts of my definition of success involve winning the Pulitzer Prize (sigh, not there yet), having a host of happy clients, being a good dog-mom, and creating a giant garden.

Can our definition of success change? Yes. Perhaps it changes as our life situation changes or as we learn new things or as we accomplish important goals or age. Let it change. Examine what has changed. Then redefine success.

Take a Motivation Assessment

Consider taking a test designed to help you better understand what motivates you on an unconscious level. I use the online PRINT Survey questionnaire at www.paulhertzgroup.com. The results indicate what unconsciously motivates us, such as being appreciated, being correct, being strong and self-reliant, being successful, being knowledgeable, being safe, being unique, or enjoying life.

The PRINT Survey indicated that I am motivated by enjoying life and being self-reliant. I won't hang around a job if I'm bored. Same with my client, Toby.

Toby loved his government job at first. However, four years in, he was bored, felt listless, and watched the clock. It seemed to me that he had a passive I-don't-care attitude. Toby took the PRINT Survey and learned his unconscious motivator was to enjoy life. He thrived on change and the new and different. He also discovered that he excelled at innovation. He would never be happy at a job grounded in tradition. He couldn't leave his job right away because he needed to support his family. I asked Toby to develop a long-range plan to slowly transition into a more interesting career. He began volunteering as a consultant who advised startups about government contracting opportunities. Then, he took on a few consulting gigs on the weekends. He eventually left his government job to start his own consulting company. He also became an expert in mitigating risk for startups.

Review: Know What Motivates You

Tools	Things to think about
Look for evidence	What has motivated you in the past?
Define success	What is your personal definition of success?
Take a motivation assessment	If you took a motivation test, what was the result?

Know Your Strengths

Knowing what your strengths are, especially as an outlier, will help you believe in yourself and have faith in your ideas when no one else does.

Determine What You Do Good

Jerome came to me saying, "I suck at details." He is the CEO of a non-profit organization and excels at strategy, long-range planning, forming alliances, public relations, and leading change. He struggles with details, such as managing a calendar and reviewing long reports. He even struggles if he has to hear details. I asked if he'd rather focus on his strengths. At that time, Jerome was asked to facilitate an alliance for about 100 nonprofits. He started to focus on his strengths of strategic vision and public relations and proceeded to lay the groundwork for the new alliance. Jerome began to surround himself with *detail people* who not only managed the details but excelled at it. Jerome later told me, "I still suck at details, but I'm damn good at what I do good."

The idea is to know yourself well enough so that you can focus on what you do best. What are your strengths? If you're not sure, ask yourself what you *do good*, as Jerome would say. But sometimes, it is complicated to figure out what we *do good*.

Ask Others

Asking others about your strengths can be an awkward thing. It can feel arrogant or embarrassing. The typical documentation that people often use to identify strengths—performance evaluations and 360 evaluations—have their uses but are more often useless.

Consider being a spy. Observe where and when you get compliments. Identify what others consistently ask you to do. When do others ask your opinion? What tasks does your boss seem to consistently assign you?

Perhaps you are OK asking others. Go ahead and just ask. What are my strengths? Be prepared to listen, be surprised, and be gracious if you don't like what you hear.

What Do You Enjoy?

My husband, Ken, likes to look at things, take them apart, learn how they work, and put them back together. When he was a child, his father brought home bags of broken electronic toys. He told Ken, "If you can fix them, you can have them." Ken enjoyed analyzing why the toy was broken, problem-solving, and then repairing the toy. His strengths are analysis and problem-solving. Today, he is an engineer. What do you enjoy?

What Did You Do as a Child?

Ken's story started as fun in childhood. What we did for fun as a child can inform our present. I taught school to stuffed animals and wrote stories. I am now an instructional designer, writer, and coach. My client Bill created machines out of Legos. He is now a mechanical engineer. Another client, Lee, raised miniature pigs when she was a teen. She is now a veterinarian.

What did you do as a child? It may provide insight about what your strengths are today.

Review: Know Your Strengths

Tools	Things to think about
Determine what you *do good*	What activities, skills, or tasks do you do well?
Ask others	What types of things do other people ask you to do or ask you for help with?
What do you enjoy?	As an adult, what do you like to do?
What did you do as a child?	As a child, what did you like to do?

Know How You Communicate

We all communicate differently, and if we are aware of how we communicate, we may better understand why people react to us the way they do. It will also give us the power to adjust our communication style to better convey our ideas. This is especially good for outliers who sometimes inadvertently offend others or misrepresent ourselves.

Observe Your Impact on Others

How do we communicate? How do we talk to people? Tabitha communicated in short telegraph-like sentences, bordering on abrasive. She didn't use social niceties, such as how-are-you or hello or some other greeting.

She even considered her name too long and prefers to be called Tab in lieu of Tabitha. I appreciate this type of communication style, but Dean didn't.

Dean is the opposite of Tabitha. He communicates with lots of words, niceties, and smoothness. Imagine the following conversation Dean described.

"Hi, Tab," Dean says. "Could you crunch these numbers for me? They're for the Adams report and the boss wants them this week."

"Sure," Tabitha says.

"I wouldn't ask, but the boss moved the deadline up and I have to get the rest of the report ready."

"Got it," Tabitha says.

"And you're so good with the analysis piece," Dean says.

"I said I got it," Tabitha says.

I was asked to group coach the team that included Dean and Tabitha. During the session, Dean told the group he felt Tabitha was cold and aloof. Tabitha claimed that Dean was overly sensitive. Other team members voiced similar concerns, not about Dean and Tabitha, but about other members in the team. Nobody seemed to have any idea about the impact they had on others.

Everyone has their own communication style. Everyone probably thinks their style is the best or even the only style. If we discover people are consistently responding to us in an unfavorable way, we should consider ourselves first.

Observe how you talk to people. How do you begin and end a conversation? Listen to yourself talk on the phone. Notice how you ask questions or make requests or give directions or orders. You're looking for your impact. Observe how people respond to you. Notice when they respond in a negative way. Notice when they respond in a positive way. In turn, notice how you respond.

Watch how other people talk to each other. Yes, go ahead and eavesdrop. Notice any rituals of communication with the greeting, the small talk, or the relationship-forming.

Learn how you communicate under stress. Do you become defensive or offensive? Do you lash out and yell? Do you become impulsive and lose control over what you say? Do you clam up and say nothing? Do you get in the last word and quickly walk away?

Observe how people negotiate. Notice the jargon. Notice when the communication is elegant, when it is *rough*, when it is technical, or when it is simple. Watch for the rituals of communication specific to negotiation, such as giving acknowledgment.

I communicate like a farm girl. I don't like lots of adjectives or adverbs. When people talk to me, I will mentally delete the adjectives and adverbs.

Review: Know How You Communicate

Tool	Things to think about
Observe your impact on others	When do people respond favorably to you? When do people respond negatively to you? How do you respond under stress?

Know Your Temperament

Don't be confused between what people say you are and who you know you are.

—Oprah Winfrey

Gloria and Sally work together. They came to me for coaching on how to better work together. Gloria is an extroverted, strategic, big-picture thinker, and makes fast decisions. Her pet peeve is when other people take too long to make decisions, at which point she becomes irritable, impatient, and bullyish. Sally is an introverted, analytical thinker, careful, and concerned with details. She wants to assess the data before deciding. Her pet peeve is when other people push her to make a fast decision before she has had time to study the data, at which point she becomes withdrawn and stubborn. The moment Gloria and Sally voiced these things, they understood how their temperaments differed. I was amazed they had not realized this sooner. Gloria now asks Sally how much time she needs and gives her that time. Sally now gives Gloria updates and, for special projects, will work faster.

Learn About Temperament

Temperament is our nature, our behavior, and how we respond to others when pushed. Temperament includes our characteristics, our uniqueness, and how we are different from others. Some scientists say we are born with temperament. It is a genetic trait, such as extrovert versus introvert. Temperament is also related to personality. If we are born with our temperament, other scientists say we develop our personality through our life experience.

Tests can help us learn about both our temperament and personality, though they are not usually called tests. They are often referred to as inventories, indexes, quotients, surveys, or questionnaires. Examples include the following:

- The Keirsey Temperament Sorter (helps us learn about our temperament type, with a focus on behavior)
- The Myers–Briggs-Type Indicator (helps us identify some of our personal preferences, such as introvert versus extrovert)
- The Holland Codes (helps match us with career choices based on personality)

Most of these tests must be taken through a certified administrator and are not free. You can sometimes find free or shortened versions of some of the tests on the Internet, which can be fun and informative.

Beware: Personality and temperament tests are not the final word on who you are. They are not rules. They are not ancient wisdom. They simply provide information and allow us to look at ourselves in different ways. The tests can be inaccurate, even deceiving, for many reasons, such as cultural bias or changing mores or the test-taker knows how to manipulate the test. There is no rule that you must agree with any of them. After taking a test, notice what resonates with you. What doesn't?

Bake a Cake

It's odd and not scientific, but it works. Describe how you would bake a cake. How do you plan the cake? Do you need a photograph of the finished cake? (I need a photograph.) Do you quickly scan the recipe to make sure you know what to do? If yes to any of these, think of yourself as a big-picture, strategic personality, perhaps a bit on the spontaneous side. Or, do you carefully read the recipe, check to see if you have all the ingredients, and double-check expiration dates?

How do you mix the cake? Do you bring out the ingredients as you need them? If you discover you are missing an ingredient, do you figure out a substitute? Do you sometimes eyeball a measurement in lieu of actually measuring? If yes, you tend to be creative, more flexible, and perhaps resilient.

Or, do you gather all the ingredients, utensils, pans, bowls, and mixers? What if you are missing an ingredient? No, you wouldn't have missing ingredients because you double-checked earlier. Do you measure carefully with separate measures for liquid and dry ingredients? If yes to some of these, you tend to be a planner, are good at details, and often enjoy the process as much as creating the product.

How do you conduct the baking? Do you use nonstick pans, pour the batter in, jiggle the pans, and then pop them into the oven? Do you note the clock on the wall and make a mental note when the cake will be done, or do you touch the cake or wait until you smell the cake to know it's done? If yes to any of these, think of yourself as more intuitive and perceptive, even sensory, perhaps in touch with nature. You might have a minimalist attitude that leans toward efficiency.

Or, do you preheat the oven, perhaps checking for hotspots? Do you butter, flour, and line the cake pans and measure the same amount of batter for each pan, then even out the batter with an inverted spatula? Do you use a timer and test for doneness with a toothpick? If any of this describes you, think of yourself as good with evaluation or adhering to criteria in order to achieve a result.

Each phase of the process will reveal a hidden gem about you. Then, have cake and celebrate. Don't forget to add chocolate frosting.

Review: Know Your Temperament

Tools	Things to think about
Learn about temperament	How would you describe your temperament?
Bake a cake	Describe how you would bake a cake. What does it say about you?

Know Your Business Self

Know thyself: the entrepreneur's secret weapon.

—**Brian Clark**

To be successful in business, no matter what our position is, we've got to know how we handle risks, failure, and setbacks, and especially, what our leadership style is. This is all part of our business self.

What Is Your Leadership Style?

We can start by learning how we function and respond as leaders. This applies to all manner of work, whether in the corporate, small business, or entrepreneurial world. It applies even if we are not in leadership positions, for we are leaders of how we do our individual work.

What is leadership? There are countless definitions, though I am going to define *leadership* as the ability to influence others. There are countless theories and models of leadership. Here are the basic types of leadership theory:

- Great man theory: Leaders are born to accomplish great things and fulfill a destiny.
- Trait theory: Leaders are people who possess certain traits, such as honesty, courage, visionary thinking.
- Transactional theory: Leaders are in a transaction with their employees, getting something in return, such as doing work for a paycheck.
- Transformational theory: Leaders inspire others and get their voluntary commitment toward a shared goal or vision, often focused on change.
- Contingency theory: Leaders adapt to the overall situation and adjust their style to meet the specific needs of the situation or the people involved.
- Servant model: Leaders serve the needs of the employees, such as helping them grow professionally and personally.

The key to leadership is that there is no one best leadership theory. Sometimes, we have to switch it up. Craig retired as a lieutenant colonel after a 20-year career with the military. For his second career, he accepted an offer to be the director of a company that created training programs for emergency response personnel. He came to me for coaching on how to adjust to this new career.

Craig had passion for the work, but it became a painful truth for him that his former transactional leadership style of giving orders was not going to be successful or even useful. The staff, mostly civilians, seemed to operate in a different world than Craig. The e-learning department was especially foreign to him. It was in a dark basement full of extremely young people talking in technical jargon. When he gave an order, they sometimes politely refused (yes, they explained why). Conflict after conflict occurred between him and the staff.

Craig came to coaching devastated. He thought he was a good leader. Something was wrong, he said. He had attended leadership schools while in the military, but that world was made up of military troops who followed orders. Craig's strength turned out to be talent development. He was used to training troops, getting them promoted, and then training new troops. He started focusing on training and developing his civilian staff. He took on the more collaborative servant model approach. He took courses on emotional intelligence. He took assessments and participated in leadership workshops. What was his big takeaway? "Know your leadership style and then adapt your style to fit the people and mission you are supposed to lead."

There are other ways to learn about leadership style. Read biographies, autobiographies, and memoirs of the people you admire. They are usually not written in the leadership genre, but they often provide nuggets of leadership wisdom. I like the following books:

- *Mary Kay: The Success Story of America's Most Dynamic Businesswoman,* by Mary Kay Ash
- *Long Walk to Freedom: The Autobiography of Nelson Mandela,* by Nelson Mandela
- *Hannibal,* by Ernle Bradford
- *The Story of George Washington Carver,* by Eva Moore
- *Night,* by Elie Wiesel

Watch more movies. Again, the movies are not usually produced specifically to illustrate leadership, but they often do illustrate different aspects of leadership (and nonleadership). Movies I like include:

- *The Bridge on the River Kwai*
- *We Were Soldiers*

- *The King's Speech*
- *Apollo 13*
- *Invictus*
- *Star Trek (any of them)*

Know How You Recover From Mistakes and Failures

We are human, and therefore make mistakes and experience failure. Do we know how we respond to them? Do mistakes and failure devastate us? Or, can we recover? Is recovery a reflective process? Or, does it involve a beer and better-luck-next-time attitude? Some people get right back on the horse and try again. Some are depressed for weeks. It is important to know how we respond in the face of mistakes and failure because it has an impact on those we lead. How we recover from failures and mistakes will set the example for others to follow. If we make a mistake, try to learn from it, and try again, our team will do the same.

My favorite failure happened when I was working as the safety officer at a state mental hospital in Columbus, Georgia. I was faced with two huge projects. I had time for only one. I chose the most urgent project and ignored the other. No, I didn't have the good sense to renegotiate the second project. I excelled at the urgent project and made the hospital look good. The day came when I had to face Gladys, the director of nursing, and admit that I had ignored her project. In front of all, I admitted my failure and apologized. Gladys looked over at me and simply said, "Welcome to the human race." Then, she asked her staff to assist me with the project. Thank you, Gladys!

How we respond to mistakes and failure can fuel or destroy the spirit of innovation. If innovation is critical to your business, find a way to professionally deal with mistakes, such as lessons-learned sessions, a think-tank, or an innovation lab.

Know Your Tolerance for Risk

For our purposes here, I am going to define *risk tolerance* as our ability to deal with the possibility of loss. Taking risks is often part of business. Risks could include how we invest, advertise, and hire, and what projects we accept. Almost all businesses involve some element of risk. There is really no such thing as business as usual.

Do you know how much risk you can tolerate? One clue can be your gas tank. When do you fill up? Half empty? When the red light comes on? Ten miles after the red light comes on, and then turning off the air conditioner or heater and coasting on the downhills to allegedly save fuel?

If you learn you have little tolerance for risk, don't try a startup. Don't go after your own business. Don't go into real estate, sales, or any other business where there is a higher level of uncertainty.

How about your job? Suppose you are assigned a large, expensive project. What is the impact if the project fails? If it does, a lessons-learned session about the failure is not going to save the company or your job. How about a job or career change? As a career coach, I would be remiss if I didn't discuss risk with my clients as it relates to career change. Sometimes a client has a high risk tolerance, but their situation does not. It could be disastrous if a single mom whose only income was from waiting tables quit her waitress job today to seek her fortune as an artist. We would talk about risk first. We would talk about how to manage the risk second.

The classic methods to mitigate risk usually involve a risk assessment and a detailed risk management plan. Here is a simplified method:

- Identify the consequences if you fail.
- Do your research (funding, expertise, potential market).
- Have a Plan A.
- Have a Plan B (contingency plan).
- Stay focused on the outcome.
- Stay relevant (you may have to reinvent the business or learn new skills).

Review: Know Your Business Self

Tools	Things to think about
Understand your leadership style	Describe your leadership style. Describe a time when your leadership style didn't work. What might have worked better?
Recover from mistakes and failure	Describe a failure in your life. How did you recover from that failure?
Know your tolerance for risk	If you own a car, describe when you typically fill the tank. What type of risk do you encounter at your workplace? How do you manage risk at your workplace?

Know Your Blind Spots

Know thyself? If I knew myself, I'd run away.

—Johann Wolfgang von Goethe

Blind spots are our preferences, biases, and inherent prejudices. We all have them. Blind spots can potentially cloud our perspective of ourselves and cause us to behave poorly. They often are in stealth mode. We don't see them and remain unaware of their presence. But, they are present and interfere with our lives.

Know How You Give Credit

Think about the last victory you experienced. What credit did you take? If it included others, did you give them credit? If not, you are a victim of self-serving bias. This blind spot is a way of thinking that makes a person see themselves in an overly favorable manner. It's this person who continually claims all the credit for success.

My suggestion is to always give credit to others. This is especially true when you are in a leadership position. Give all the credit to the staff. Think about that victory as an award, and part of your acceptance speech is to give credit and thank others. This is so true in business. Give credit. A leader or manager or boss has no business taking the credit unless it is on behalf of the troops or the staff or the workers.

Know Your Prejudice and Behave

We all have our personal prejudice. If we think we have no prejudice, we are either naïve or an idiot. What is your prejudice? Identify it. Learn about it. My prejudice? Pregnant women. I was scared to write this and cringed when I did. My editor said she cringed when she read it. I hate to admit it, but in the spirit of transparency and honesty, I do admit it. I'm sorry ladies. It started when I was in the Army. When a female soldier got pregnant, she was pulled from regular duty. Someone else had to fill the gap. Often it was me. Between light duty and maternity leave, that female soldier was not available for regular duty for over a year. Later, as a manager and director, I experienced the same with female civilian staff. Always the pregnant female got special treatment. I came to resent pregnant females.

Do I get to justify my prejudice? No. Do I get to manifest it? No. Do I get to preach my prejudice? No. I get to identify it, and then behave in a respectful manner. To never allow that prejudice to interfere. I even wondered if, as a female, I was perhaps jealous of pregnant women. I had decided, after all, not to have children myself. It didn't matter. I had to keep that prejudice swallowed up and managed so that I could allow respectful behavior to grow and hopefully become authentic. To my knowledge, I never allowed that prejudice to interfere with how I treated a pregnant lady. Not once.

Then I came to understand that all employees get special treatment sooner or later. One staff member wanted to come to work an hour late so he could exercise every morning. Another person needed to work from home once a week to take care of kids. Someone else went on a six-month sabbatical. And, someone else got to cross-train in another department she was interested in. My administrative assistant and I both left work early twice a week to go to school. Every one of my staff got some type of special treatment. Wow, what a motivated staff that was! I still feel fortunate that I was able to make that happen. Thank you, pregnant ladies.

Know your prejudice and behave.

Know Your Hot Buttons

A hot button is something that causes us to behave poorly. You might hear someone say, "They pushed my buttons." My friend John has a hot button about incorrect grammar, spelling, or language use. He corrects the e-mails he receives from colleagues and returns them. This irritates some people. I find it charming. Clients Vince and Tomas have hot buttons concerning people who arrive late to meetings. Vince is a fire safety instructor and locks the door when he starts class. Ironically, this may be a safety violation. Tomas is a chief financial officer, and when conducting a meeting, he will point out the late person with passive-aggressive comments such as, "I hope our meeting didn't interfere with your coffee break." Another client, Annie, has a hot button dealing with disorganization. When she comes to your office, she will start to organize the stuff on your desk. Seraz, a colleague, has a hot button about people who don't have a positive outlook. He will debate, argue, and become defensive whenever someone says no.

How do you know if you have hot buttons? Watch for an immediate, automatic response in yourself, as if you can't control it or are protecting yourself. How do you know if you are behaving poorly? Watch for the response in other people. Are they resisting? Are they getting upset or mad? Are they, in turn, behaving poorly?

We all have hot buttons. However, if the hot buttons cause you to feel too intense or become uncontrollable or trigger a traumatic response, please seek help. There are many resources out there, such as counselors, therapists, hypnotists, spiritual leaders, support groups, and doctors. Seek them out. You are worth it. If money is an issue, some of these resources are free, such as some support groups.

Learn to know yourself...to search realistically and regularly the processes of your own mind and feelings.

— **Nelson Mandela**

Review: Know Your Blind Spots

Tools	Things to think about
Know how you give credit	In business, how do you give and take credit for a job well done? When do you withhold congratulations, kudos, or words of praise when others succeed?
Know your prejudice and behave	What are you biased against? Why do you think you have this bias? How does this bias impact your professional life? What could you do to manage this bias?
Know your hot buttons	When do you automatically and reflexively respond poorly? When do people respond poorly to you?

Before we change the world, we need to change ourselves.

—**Patrick Daniel**

Be Ready: The Universe Will Test You

The universe will test us. One day, we will be asked to prove ourselves, to stand up, and defend our values. Life is not all fluff and goodness. There are challenges and heartbreak and unfairness. There is stress. There is disappointment. There is death. All these things can tempt or test us. And, we probably won't be tested in any expected way.

I value life. It is precious. Each person is precious. Each creature is precious. For both, I wish life. The universe tested me when my mom died. I had to decide when to stop treatment. She was suffering as her heart valves failed. She asked for my cappuccino and apple fritter, which she consumed with gusto between gurgling breaths. Then, she touched my hand. I gave permission to stop treatment, to administer the morphine to ease any pain and Ativan to ease anxiety. I held her hand until her last heart valve stopped working. What I remember most is how she relished the coffee and fritter. A perfect last supper.

Have no doubt, the universe will test you.

CHAPTER 2

Develop Courage

What would life be if we had no courage to attempt anything?

—Vincent Van Gogh

We are told to have courage when the stakes are high, when we are in the minority, when danger arises, when standing up for our values, and on and on. *Have courage.* It's a rallying cry before the battle. It's the stuff of motivational posters. "All our dreams can come true, if we have the courage to pursue them," Walt Disney said. It is the key to self-actualization. "It takes courage to grow up and become who you really are," E. E. Cummings said. It is the pathway to saving the world. "You will never do anything in this world without courage; it is the greatest quality of the mind next to honor," said Aristotle.

Develop Courage: What Does It Mean?

One isn't necessarily born with courage, but one is born with potential. Without courage, we cannot practice any other virtue with consistency. We can't be kind, true, merciful, generous or honest.

—**Maya Angelou**

Courage is not something we are born with. However, we can develop it. Think of it as growing it within ourselves. But, what is courage? I define *courage* as the ability to do something when we are afraid. There are many definitions of courage. There is even a distinction between physical and moral courage. Oxford Living Dictionaries defines *courage* as "the ability to do something that frightens one: bravery." Merriam-Webster defines *courage* as the "mental or moral strength to venture, persevere, and withstand danger, fear, or difficulty." The Collins English Dictionary defines *courage* as "the quality shown by someone who decides to do something difficult or dangerous, even though they may be afraid." Physical courage is bravery in the face of physical pain, hardship, death, or threat of death. Moral courage is the ability to act rightly in the face of popular opposition, shame, scandal, discouragement, or personal loss. However you define it, courage is the choice we make when we are afraid.

Let's get one thing straight. Fear is OK. In some cases, fear can be a good thing and can keep us safe. You'll hear that theme throughout this chapter. We all feel fear at different points and in different situations. It's what we do in the presence of fear or how fear impacts our life that is important. It's that choice.

To develop courage means to acknowledge we are not necessarily born with it and to begin the journey to grow courage within ourselves. Yes, courage can be developed and learned.

Develop Courage: Why?

I learned that courage was not the absence of fear, but the triumph over it. The brave man is not he who does not feel afraid, but he who conquers that fear.

—Nelson Mandela

Courage is essential for the outlier. Courage helps us lead our life not by other people's expectations, but by what we want and what we think is right. Courage bolsters our confidence and allows us to go well beyond whatever expectations we might have had for ourselves in terms of accomplishment and experience. It also sets us up to be prepared for the unexpected.

Chinye worked in human resources for the U.S. Forest Service. She was terrified to say no to her boss, though she was in a high-ranking position. As a consequence, her boss ended up assigning her so much work that she basically lived at the office. She would even spend most weekends there. But, despite her desire for a life outside of work, Chinye turned pale at the thought of standing her ground and setting boundaries with her boss. She was terrified that she would get fired if she asserted herself, and she was sure that he would think less of her. She was trained as a young person to respect all authority and interpreted that to mean that she had to do everything that was asked of her, no matter how unreasonable.

It took at least six months of our working together before Chinye was able to find an authentic and workable approach to setting boundaries with her boss. She decided she wasn't going to say no to him; instead she was going to say, "Yes, *but*...I'll need to put this other project aside for now while I'm completing that task." The first time she answered her boss this way, she was shaking and threw up in the bathroom after their conversation. However, after she had some practice asserting herself, she began to gain confidence, and the relationship between her and her boss improved.

Here is an example of an entirely different situation in which courage allowed me to go beyond what I thought I was able to do. My husband (who pilots his own small plane) and I were flying from New Mexico to Florida when we hit terrible weather as we were preparing to land. We were completely socked in with clouds all around. My husband watched his instruments and talked to the tower, but I sat beside him shaking with fear, trying unsuccessfully to stay calm by reading a book. My vertigo was so bad, I started to panic. My husband had taught me that even though my instincts were telling me I was upside-down, I was not. And, I'd also learned to use deep breathing exercises to quell panic, so I closed my eyes and started to slowly and rhythmically inhale and exhale. I was able to relax and sit there quietly reading my book (for real) until we were able to land safely.

This was not necessarily a life-or-death situation, but if I had let my fear get the better of me, I would have distracted my husband and possibly caused him to misjudge his calculations for landing. If I hadn't known what to expect and hadn't been prepared for a situation like that, I might've freaked out completely, which would have definitely caused a problem. I will talk more about being prepared later on in this chapter, but this experience demonstrates that developing courage can help us meet the unexpected.

Identify the Fear

There are no secrets to success. It is the result of preparation, hard work, and learning from failure.

—Colin Powell

What could we be afraid of? It might be:

- A life-threatening danger
- Failure
- Refusal

- Rejection
- Loss of job, status, or money
- Looking stupid
- The unknown
- Getting our feelings hurt
- Feeling unsafe
- Being perceived as different from other people
- Having to admit failure
- Being faced with a new situation
- Starting over
- Saying no
- Looking at a risky endeavor
- Entering a high-stakes conversation
- Requesting major support, such as a loan or investment
- Seeking a new opportunity
- Trusting someone
- Asking for help
- Learning something new, such as public speaking

Study this list and ask yourself if you can relate to any of these fears. Then ask, "What about this is fearful for me?" This may help identify the actual fear. My fear was not fitting in, which directly relates to the fear of being perceived as different from other people, the fear of rejection, and possibly the fear of looking stupid.

In the documentary *Man on Wire*, high-wire artist Philippe Petit walks a wire between the twin towers of the World Trade Center in New York City in 1974. His wire was 1,312 feet (a quarter mile) above the ground! A feat that would probably strike fear in most people. Yet, throughout the documentary, Petit does not focus on fear. He refers to his high-wire work as performance art. "There is a beauty up there," he said. "Poetry." What takes courage will be different for every individual. And, each of us needs to know what that is.

Caution: Do not confuse courage with naiveté. To go blindly into something is not courage. Do not confuse courage with the bravery soldiers or police officers display. They are trained to do that. Do not confuse fear with an adrenalin rush, such as when bungee jumping off a tall bridge. Some folks consider that fun. Then there is Philippe Petit. Do not confuse the poetry of dangerous performance with courage. That was the challenge of art by a skilled artist.

Prepare

Victory is the child of preparation and determination. You'll know how to respond during challenging circumstances to obtain a positive outcome.

—Sean Hampton

Be as prepared as you can possibly be. Be overprepared. What is the first thing movie action heroes do when they are about to embark on a dangerous mission? They get ready. What do astronauts do prior to a space flight? They spend months, if not years, getting ready.

There is no better confidence-building, courage-garnering mechanism than being well-prepared. For a presentation, the preparation could involve organizing talking points, preparing slides or handouts, rehearsing, getting the timing right, anticipating questions, or even the more minute details of gestures or what to wear. Exactly how we prepare and how much depends on the situation. I know people who say they work better without preparing, they perform best at the last minute when under stress. Good for them. But, it's probably either not true or the performance is not important to them.

Take Small Bites

So, if you're willing to make that first step, you have already made the most difficult decision there is to make.

—Martin Luther King Jr.

If you were scared of swimming and pushed to learn to swim in the deep ocean, you would probably think, "Oh my God, I can't do it." But if you got into a small pool that was only three feet deep, you would be able to overcome your fear and learn to swim. We don't normally teach someone to swim by throwing them in the deep end. When you build courage one little bit at a time, you gain the confidence to keep going and growing, learning, and progressing, until, lo and behold, you're swimming!

The lesson here is to take courage in small bites. Perhaps superheroes become mighty and courageous in the magic moment they are transformed into heroes, but that is not the way of the real world. I also have a hunch that courage is not a matter of having courage or not having courage. There are many levels of courage, more like a continuum. Plus, courage is probably situational. We may have courage in one situation, such as defending a child, and no small bites are needed. We might not have courage in another situation, such as standing up to our boss, and we may need to learn that courage in small bites.

Practice

Practice is essential if you are to be prepared for anything. Consider practice as a rehearsal. The more you practice, the more you will be armed with the appropriate skills you need when the time comes for you to have courage. Practice will generally make you more confident and prepared, but it will also give you information about what you are good at (or not) and what you enjoy (or don't).

If you discover, like I did when I took Aikido lessons, that you are simply not good at something and no amount of practice is going to change that, move on, put your attention elsewhere. I hung in there for 13 weeks of Aikido. I came to dread it more with every practice. I didn't understand the moves and follow-through, and struggled with the rolls. Finally, I moved on to Tai Chi.

We will talk about specific types of practice in the next chapter.

Focus

Have you ever experienced *butterflies* right before something important was about to happen? Perhaps you were about to make a critical presentation or go on stage or engage in a high-stakes conversation. Feeling scared is a perfectly natural response related to the release of cortisol and adrenalin when our bodies or minds perceive a threat. If you get the butterflies, whatever you are about to do is probably important to you. Fortunately, this butterfly response is necessary for peak performance. The adrenalin and cortisol keep us alert.

When we feel the butterflies, it's time to become alert and get focused. How? Try experimenting with the following focusing suggestions:

- Know what you believe in
- Know what you want
- Slow down
- Breathe slowly
- Momentarily delete everything else in your brain, except your mission

When the butterflies come, it is not the time to whine or dwell on the fact we are nervous. It's not time to worry about what others will say or do. It's not time to seek refuge or solace in others or to be babied or coddled. It is time for us to become alert and get focused. This, in turn, will help us perform well.

When I was in the Army, I attended jump school where I learned how to jump out of airplanes. Right before we were to make the first jump, a jumpmaster asked me if I was nervous. I was only one of three women in a company of 200. The other two women said, "No, no! Not at all!" But I said, "Hell, yeah! I'm terrified." The jumpmaster said, "Good. You better be. Your fear will keep you safe." He said he still got the butterflies every time he jumped, even though he'd jumped hundreds of times. "Now, get focused," the jumpmaster said.

Have a Plan B

There are times when there is only one course of action, only one chance, and only one way out. Fortunately, that usually only happens in the movies. If you find yourself in a situation with only one terrifying course of action, then skip to the next section and *do something*.

In most cases, you will be able to develop a backup plan. Backup plans include contingency plans, optional plans, or alternative plans that address unexpected situations. You will gain more power when you know what to do if Plan A doesn't work. Having a backup plan will help you act confidently and go forward without hesitation.

It may also be helpful to know when to move to other options. Is it immediately after Plan A doesn't work? Is a waiting or reflecting time needed? Is there a list of criteria that needs to be met? Backup plans can also include retreat or exit plans and knowing when to get out of dodge.

In businesses, backup plans usually include continuity plans, crisis management, asset protection, transition or reorganization plans, violence-in-the-workplace plans, and scenario planning. These are typically formal plans practiced in the organization to ensure the organization stays safe or continues to function. Small businesses often neglect these plans and should at least look at a backup plan if something should happen to the business owner. Startups are usually concerned with getting launched successfully and should probably focus on backup plans involving funding, marketing, getting customers, or unexpected expenses.

Backup plans can help you address the *black swan*, otherwise known as the worst-case scenario. Consider the famous case study of Royal Dutch Shell. The company survived the oil crisis disaster in the late 1960s and early 1970s by identifying their potential black swan, which was the possibility of oil prices collapsing. Through their scenario planning process, they knew if that happened and they didn't have a contingency plan, they would go out of business. When the black swan emerged and oil prices collapsed, they dug up their Plan B, dusted it off, and pivoted. They sold off excess oil reserves when other companies were buying. This move saved Royal Dutch Shell, and they survived the oil crisis.

Companies must always be on the lookout for the situations that could put them out of business. They must have a Plan B. Yes, it takes courage to imagine the unimaginable, the black swan. But, if we can muster the courage and create a Plan B in advance of any crisis, we don't have to be scared. We can go direct to Plan B without hesitation.

In our personal lives, backup plans might involve an emergency fund, layoffs, the slow start of a new business, what to spend money and time on, and what not to. Having a backup plan allows us to continue, know how to respond, and respond with a measure of courage when the universe puts obstacles in our path.

Self-Care

One aspect of preparation that is often overlooked is self-care. Believe it or not, it does make a difference. If you're taking care of your diet, if you're getting enough exercise, if you're doing breath work or yoga or have some other way to relax, you will be able to calm yourself in the face of nerves. You will be able to sleep better, which is crucial to cultivating calm, staying focused, and facing stressful or frightening situations.

Review: Prepare

Tools	Things to think about
Take small bites	Identify a fear you want to overcome. Create a list of 10 steps (10 small bites) that might help you overcome the fear.
Practice	Identify something that scares you. How could you practice or rehearse doing it? For example, the client who was afraid to say no to her boss rehearsed many times how she could respond to him.
Focus	Identify the most important thing in your life. How can you focus on this when you are afraid? The next time you're afraid, agitated, or overemotional, experiment with breathing slowly.
Have a Plan B	If you lost your job today, what would you do?
Self-care	What is one way you can take better care of yourself?

Do Something

Inaction breeds doubt and fear. Action breeds confidence and courage. If you want to conquer fear, do not sit home and think about it. Go out and get busy.

—Dale Carnegie

There are times when we must take action. When we must summon up whatever courage we have and go for it. When we must do something. Perhaps we don't think about it. Perhaps we simply have to pretend we have courage. This may not be a bad thing. Sometimes the act of doing or pretending will generate an element of courage.

Take Forward Action

I once heard a speaker tell a fable about the bunny that almost died of fear. When wild bunnies are scared or trying to hide, they often freeze and pretend they're a rock in the hope that the predator won't see them. The bunny curled into a rock, and froze, terrified to move. The bunny became stuck that way until a traveler, who watched it for a time, poked it gently with a little stick. The stick startled the bunny into action, and it finally uncurled itself and scampered away.

Take any positive forward action. Take a walk. Think about it. Talk about it, read about it. Take action that will get you moving in the direction you want to be going, especially if you're afraid. That will disrupt the paralysis of fear. Poke the bunny!

Do Something With a Team

> *When spider webs unite, they can tie up a lion.*
>
> **—Ethiopian proverb**

Sometimes, a team can help us develop courage. It could be a formal team with defined roles and tasks. Or, it could be an informal team such as a group of like-minded persons participating in a community service project. It could also be a team of just two people. The key concept to a team is to have other people to talk to. People with whom we can brainstorm new concepts, develop solutions and contingency plans, share concerns or fears, practice, or confront potential obstacles. This exchange can have a synergistic and courage-bolstering effect.

When putting together a team, first, look for people who are different than you, think differently than you, even disagree with you. If you surround yourself with people like yourself, it just becomes a narcissistic exercise. Or, you will end up with a team of folks who coddle each other. Second, the team members need to learn how to communicate with each other. Everyone sends and receives communication differently. Figure all that out before calling the team a team. Third, develop trust in your teammates.

The dark side of gathering courage from a group is peer pressure or groupthink. This emerges when someone is so afraid of the group's disapproval or rejection that this person agrees to do things they might normally not do. Beware of this.

Review: Do Something

Tools	Things to think about
Take forward action	Describe a time when you did nothing and how you wish you would have acted. What are your thoughts on pretending to have courage: the fake-it-until-you-make-it technique?
Do something with a team	Describe how working with a team impacts you. When would working with a team help you bolster courage?

Know Your Limitations

We have to confront ourselves. Do we like what we see in the mirror? And, according to our light, according to our understanding, according to our courage, we will have to say yea or nay—and rise!

—Maya Angelou

We must know ourselves well enough to know our limitations and have the courage to know when to push through them and when to back off. It is our responsibility to protect ourselves and anyone else our actions might affect. We must also be wary of blindly going forward knowing we're afraid and yet unprepared or without the skills we need to tackle whatever it is we're moving toward. There are moments when it takes more courage to admit that we do not want to do something or do not have the training or appropriate skills to move forward.

When I was a beginning diver on vacation, one of the dive masters on our boat asked, "Who wants to go to 180 feet and who wants to stay closer to the surface?" Then, they separated the groups. I'm the kind of person who always wants to be in group number one; I wanted to go deep and meet the challenge. But I had to say, "No, I'm not going 180 feet." This is considered deep for recreational divers. I was nervous and didn't feel ready. That took a lot of courage for me to admit.

Have the courage to admit you're afraid. Although this chapter is about facing our fears and working through them, there are situations in life when it's not necessary to go full throttle. Although some of our fears may be irrational, some of them may be totally reasonable. We don't have to face every fear. If you find that pushing up against a certain fear is just impossible for you, have the courage to admit it, accept it, and live with it. We can't do everything. Not everything is available to everybody, and it's up to us to pick and choose. After years of scuba diving, I can go deep now. There is still an element of nervousness surrounding deep dives, and I don't dive deep unless I am prepared and there is a reason for it, such as a cool shipwreck.

If you have a fear of public speaking, and you don't have to be a speaker, why bother learning how to speak in front of people? But, what if you end up in a position, a job for instance, in which you're asked to make presentations in front of a group. You may want to work through that fear by perhaps joining a speaking group such as Toastmasters.

Acknowledge and Accept the Fear

I use a technique with my coaching clients who are facing a fear. I tell them to imagine a bucket in the back of their brain. And then, I encourage them to speak to their fear: "Hello, fear. How are you doing today? I know you're nervous. I know you're scared. But I can do this on my own today. I'm going to have you wait in the bucket for now and just stay out of the way." Acknowledge your fear and comfort it, don't try to eliminate it, because, the truth is, the fear will probably never go away. The more you try to repress it, the more it will control you. You can confront it, you can work with it and even through it, you can accept it, live peacefully with it, even give it a time out (in the bucket), but you cannot deny it. If fear is denied, it will come up in unexpected ways. It will trip you up and take you down when you least expect it. Make friends with your fear. That way, you will always know where it is and what it's up to.

When I was in the Army, I was afraid of combat. I was, and still am, afraid of dying. And, I was going to have to lead an entire company to desert storm. We were ready to go, but it turned out we didn't have to—it ended so fast. But, before I knew we weren't going into combat, I told my first sergeant I was afraid, and he said something similar to what my jumpmaster told me, "You better be, it'll help you keep our soldiers safer.

Don't let the fear go away." Then I stood tall before the troops, ready to deploy with my fear by my side. Accept your fear as your companion in staying safe. If you respect and really listen to your fear, it will help you make wiser, more measured decisions.

Fear can be our enemy, in that it can paralyze us like the bunny or push us to make bad and dangerous decisions, or we can choose to accept our fear and allow it to assist us or challenge us to move beyond our comfort zone.

We are complex beings, not all brave heroes or all cowards. We are somewhere in between, with our moments of courage and our moments of fear. Much like the bucket exercise, self-talk can allow us to accept ourselves in a more holistic manner:

"Fear, I see you there."

"I don't like it, but it's OK."

"Stand aside. We can talk later."

"I got this."

"I'll get through it."

Review: Know Your Limitations

Tool	Things to think about
Acknowledge and accept the fear	How do you typically manage your fear? What kind of self-talk could you engage in? What fear do you have that is not necessary for you to overcome?

Be Ready: The Universe Will Test You

Courage is not the absence of fear, but rather the judgment that something else is more important than fear.

—Ambrose Redmoon

When I was in my early 30s and had just gotten out of the Army, I moved to a quiet all-white neighborhood in Columbus, Georgia. A black family moved in down the street. The mom and dad were schoolteachers, and they had two daughters who did gymnastics. Soon after they moved in, my next-door neighbor said to me, "There goes the neighborhood. You know how *they* are." I said nothing and continued raking leaves, though I was appalled. I valued courage and believed I wasn't racist (I am half-Mexican after all), yet when tested, I did not have the courage to speak up.

In that moment, I wanted to be accepted more than I valued standing up for my values. In this case, the value was courage. I was afraid of being rejected, of not fitting in, of being ostracized. Though I valued courage, this was an ironic moment when having the courage to stand up and speak up for the rights of others was terrifying. And, the moment was compounded by my fear of not fitting in. I was tired of not fitting in. I wanted my neighbor to accept me. I said nothing, and the neighbor seemed to approve.

In that same moment of my silence, I recognized my consent and cowardice. I was complicit in an act of prejudice. I vowed never to let it happen again. Bravery is the capacity to behave ethically, according to your values, according to what is important, even when scared. I now understand that courage is more important than fitting in.

You will be tested. You may pass the test or you may not. You too may vow to *never let it happen again.*

Bravery is the capacity to perform properly even when scared half to death.

—Omar N. Bradley

CHAPTER 3

Develop Mastery

If people knew how hard I worked to get my mastery, it wouldn't seem so wonderful at all.

—**Michelangelo**

What Is Mastery?

What do you want to be when you grow up? I never really had an answer to this question. My sister Jan knew she wanted to be an engineer when she was in the seventh grade. My husband, Ken, knew he wanted to be an engineer at a very young age. Perhaps it's an engineer thing. As a career coach, I've noticed that many of us don't know. We spend years trying to figure out what we want to be. Years trying to find a purpose or passion. Or, we muddle along.

I asked my client Terry, "What is your purpose?" She said she didn't know. "Possibly to discover a new way of being?" But she couldn't explain what that meant, only that she was unhappy with her career. At the time, she was an administrative assistant at a hospital and a single mom. I asked her, "What is your passion?" She had no answer and said she didn't understand the question. Then I asked her, "What do you want to be when you grow up?" She said, "I want to be superorganized. In fact, it's my superpower, I'm really good at it."

To be an organization superhero, Terry had to become good at it. Master it. She started simply by reorganizing her work area, then her computer files, then learned a basic management system, then a task system, then a project tracking system. She took classes using the tuition remission and training offered by the hospital. She got promoted to project coordinator. At home, she reorganized her house and eliminated all clutter, except for toys. She made it easy to find stuff. Her rule became, "If I can't find it in 30 seconds, there is something wrong." She organized chores and created weekly menus with the kids. She soon had more time. She could do more fun things with the kids. With her promotion, she could finally afford to go to college.

It's been four years, and Terry will graduate next year with a business degree in management. She's been promoted again, to project manager, and has become known for her organizational ability. She still says she doesn't know her purpose. But, she says she is happy and will continue to hone her craft of organization until she can call herself an organization superhero.

Terry was fortunate. She knew she had this crazy, strange passion for organization. Many people don't know what they are passionate about, especially when it comes to work and career. Many folks don't have a clear idea of purpose either. I think finding our purpose, passion, or calling may be overrated. Focus on being happy. Meanwhile, my suggestion is to become good at something while trying to figure it all out. Master something.

Develop Mastery: What Does It Mean?

Mastery: the desire to get better and better at something that matters.
—**Daniel H. Pink**

I define *mastery* as the comprehensive knowledge of a subject, or acquired skill or ability, or expertise in an area of interest. To master a subject is to become among the best at it, to be able to teach it, to be able to reinterpret it, to take that subject to the level of art and amazement. When someone has mastered a skill, people gasp and ask, "How did they do that?"

Let's be clear what mastery is not. The term *mastery* or *master* may be a sensitive term in today's time of racial unrest. For our work here, mastery is not about superiority. It's not about control. It's not about domination or power over others. It's not even about power over nature.

For our purposes, mastery is simply about becoming extremely good at something. Think expert or expertise. Or virtuoso. Sensei.

Develop Mastery: Why?

A happy life consists not in the absence, but in the mastery of hardships.
—**Helen Keller**

I believe life is precious. Your life is precious. Please don't waste it. If you have a passion, or interest or natural ability, become excellent at it. Meanwhile, if you don't have that or are looking for that, find something to become good at.

Developing mastery can serve us well. It can potentially pay bills, provide us a role in society, develop our confidence, and provide a sense of accomplishment.

To develop mastery is not to become trapped by it. We can change directions, make a different turn in our life journey at any time. To become good at something can be the starting point. It can be the inspiration that leads us to something different.

If our passion or purpose (when we find it) is meant to be our Plan A, the thing we are good at could become our Plan B. I am good at instructional design, and fortunately, I like it. I can do instructional design if my dreams of writing and coaching, which I love, don't work out. It would give me a place to regroup, rethink, reinvent, and muster my resources to try again. Be careful. The Plan B approach might not work for some folks. It might distract them too long or become so comfortable that Plan A never gets a chance.

Select Something

A successful career will no longer be about promotion. It will be about mastery.

—Michael Martin Hammer

I ended up joining the Army because the Air Force was not allowing people with nontechnical degrees into their officer training program, and I wanted to go in as an officer. I selected the military not because I had a deep desire to serve in that capacity, but because it was familiar (both my father and mother were in the Air Force), and because I didn't know what to do with my creative writing degree. I had also just told a wonderful man I couldn't marry him. All I knew was that I wanted to travel, and that I had some leadership ability. I was muddling along and needed to make a decision about how to move forward with my life. I had to do something. It was a somewhat impulsive choice, but joining the Army turned out to be one of the best decisions I ever made.

The recruiter asked me what I wanted to do, and I said I wanted to be close to the combat line. I chose the Military Police. When I was finally able to put my lieutenant bars on, I felt for the first time that I had status. I felt like I was somebody. I belonged. It was a fantastic feeling. I was eventually stationed in Germany and found that I loved living in

Europe. I was there 11 years: six years as a military person, five years as a civilian.

If you don't have a clear sense of what you want, do something, anything! You may make a choice to move forward in a direction that seems somewhat random. But, you may find that you have instinctually moved toward a job or career that resonates on some deep inner level, one that may even utilize your skill set. Neither my college major nor my decision to join the Army were choices born of passion, but they were both the best decisions I ever made. The Army gave me wonderful opportunities I would never have had otherwise. And, my writing degree has finally paid off by giving me the confidence and skill to write books.

Select a Trade

I recently became aware of an artist who was basically brainwashed as a child to become an engineer, so he went into an engineering program in college. While there, he became interested in working in metal. When he graduated, instead of getting an engineering job, he went to welding school. He chose a skilled trade over the professional career he'd been trained for. A brave choice. He ultimately became such a master welder that he is now famous for his work, both as a structural welder and as a sculptor. Metal Man!

It's not necessary to go to college. Consider a skilled trade. We certainly need more people in the skilled trades. And, once you develop a mastery of it, you'll have a good living to fall back on or to take you someplace new. The skilled trades can be broken into three categories—industrial, construction, and service—and include many diverse and interesting pursuits, from welding, plumbing, and plastering, to nursing, leather work, and cooking.

Go to School

My mom always used to say, "When you don't know what to do, go back to school." This could be college or a technical program or just a class. And, these days, so many great classes and degree programs are online. Many are reasonably priced or even free. If you are interested in a degree or certificate program or a course of study that costs more money than you have on hand, many resources, loans, and work-study opportunities are now available. Don't let finances hold you back!

Start a Business

Starting a business is not for everyone, but it's a possibility, especially if you are a self-starter and have something to offer. Your business can be anything from baking cookies you sell at the local farmers market or making jewelry you sell online, to a service you offer such as copywriting or consulting. It can be a small business that brings in a little extra money or something that becomes a large business and perhaps even a lifetime pursuit. It could be a startup that you eventually sell.

Get a Job

Getting a job, especially when you need the money and have no sense of the direction you *really* want to go in, can bring you more than a paycheck. I once took a job in Togiak, Alaska, gently pushing salmon eggs through a screen to make caviar. I didn't exactly love the job, but I loved being in a new strange place where I met all kinds of interesting people.

Ask yourself what you want to get out of a job. Do you want to learn a new skill? Do you want a job just to make money so you can spend your free time learning how to play the guitar? Or, do you want the job to serve other goals, such as giving you the opportunity to go to a cool location or work with a specific chef, artist, craftsperson, academic, or professional? Be creative and even daring with your choices. The job you get may end up being the occupation, craft, or skill you master, or the thing that leads you to your true purpose or passion.

Send a Letter From the Future

I have many clients who say their biggest regret is that they fear they've wasted time doing jobs they didn't love. It can be tough to convince them that the time they spent experimenting with different jobs, courses of study, nonfocused pursuits, and careers was not wasted time. Unfortunately, it's often not until we are older that we are able to look back and see how all the various things we did, even the jobs we hated or did purely for the money, were not an absolute waste of time. From the vantage point of old age, we can see how the seemingly disparate paths we took came together to create the opportunities we had and the experiences that shaped us and made us who we are.

Try this exercise I sometimes give to my coaching clients. I call it "message from the future." I ask my clients to pretend they are 80 years old and request they write a letter to themselves as a younger person. In most cases, the future, older client congratulates their younger self for their tenacity and courage. The older self usually writes that they are proud of the younger self and encourages them to continue following their vision. The older self will always reassure them that they *aren't* wasting their time with whatever job they're doing, degree they're seeking, or career track they're on. They are, in fact, creating the building blocks that will eventually lead them to the position or business of their dreams. Clients usually have tears in their eyes by the end of this exercise.

Review: Select Something

Tools	Things to think about
Select a trade	What skill do you have that could possibly lead to a trade? How much does a plumber earn? How much do you earn?
Go to school	When was the last time you were in school? What would you like to learn?
Start a business	If you were to start a business, describe what it might be.
Get a job	Describe your current job. Are you happy in this job? How does this job serve you?
Send a letter from the future	Allow your 80-year-old self to five you advice.

Enjoy the Journey

We fail to realize that mastery is not about perfection. It is about a process, a journey.

—George Leonard

It was my very first day of graduate school, and I was taking a class out of order. I was supposed to take a whole bunch of introductory classes, but I was really, really hungry for this class. Our professor, Dr. Patsy Bovary, put us in a circle and had us introduce ourselves. Almost every person said, "I will be graduating at Christmastime… I will be graduating in the spring… I will be graduating in three semesters." When she got to me, I said, "This is my very first class, and I won't be graduating for a good long time." She said, "I'm so glad. I don't know why everyone is in such a hurry. Enjoy the journey!"

Her words still remind me to slow down, to enjoy the journey. Sometimes we're so anxious to get to the goal that we miss everything in between. The diploma is not important, except for job hunting and bragging rights, but the process of getting that diploma and expanding your knowledge is what's important.

Take the Time

Long ago, I worked with a team that was asked by a large company to create a program to fast-track experts. They wanted us to find a way to take people just out of college and quickly turn them into experts or masters in their fields. These people had natural ability and talent. They were passionate and learned quickly, and it was possible that they might need less time to become experts. However we chose to turn the challenge down, determining that there was no way we could produce a formula guaranteed to create an instant expert. Expertise takes time. There's just no way around it!

Toward the end of college, I remember telling my creative writing teacher that I was going to join the Army and see the world. He said, "That will be good for you. It will mature your writing." The truth was (and I knew it deep inside), my writing, though technically good, was superficial. He said, "You need to live life so you have something to write about." Change, growth, maturing, and evolving, all take time.

Celebrate

Have fun! Celebrate milestones along your journey because the journey is what's important. Celebrate your birthday, celebrate your graduation, celebrate the holidays. In other words, slow down, take the time to *smell the roses*, to acknowledge yourself. This is about honoring your accomplishments along the way, as well as celebrating those events that make life more fun. Enjoying your journey can give you the motivation to keep going, especially during the times that are extra challenging, scary, or even tedious. As my professor said, "Why is everyone in such a hurry?"

Rest

I had a weightlifting coach in Germany, a national champion, who said there were three parts to winning a competition. One was training, one was nutrition, and one was rest. He said no one was going to win a competition by working out all day, or by starving to make weight. He said you had to take time to recover. Competitive weightlifting is a good metaphor for accomplishing any goal, whether or not it's physical. You must rest to recuperate and recover your energy, focus, concentration, creativity, enthusiasm, insight, clarity, intuition, memory, and intellectual or physical prowess. Get some sleep!

Review: Enjoy the Journey

Tools	Things to think about
Take the time	What project, task, or goal, personal or professional, lies before you that will require a long time?
Celebrate	What have you celebrated in the last month?
Rest	Suppose you have two major projects that you want to complete in three months. Describe a plan for accomplishing this.

Practice

The time that leads to mastery is dependent on the intensity of our focus.

—Robert Greene

When it comes to practice, the myths abound. Some people say it takes 10,000 hours to become an expert. 5,000 hours, 20,000 hours—it's all a myth. There is no set number of hours. It differs for all of us. What matters is that you practice. And, preferably that you practice doing something you love. The 21 days to create a habit is also a myth, an observation made by a plastic surgeon.

Furthermore, practice makes perfect is not an adage to live by. What if you are practicing incorrectly or lazily? Perfect practice makes perfect is another stupid adage. There is no formula. Practice is practice. Just practice.

Practice Deliberate Practice

All practice is not created equal. There are different types of practice. In instructional design, there is a type of practice called *deliberate practice*. It's when you do something, look back at what you learned and what mistakes you made, and then refine it and keep learning.

I used to swim laps in the University of New Mexico Olympic pool, and one day while swimming, I got the chance to watch the diving team practice. The divers would climb up to the high diving platform and do their dive. As they swam back to the pool's edge, the coach would make two or three observations about their dive. Then, he would make one suggestion for them to work on during the next dive. I thought, "Interesting, he's not overloading them with a lot of feedback." The divers were able to stay focused and learn from each bit of instruction and in turn were improving noticeably with each dive. Deliberate practice is when you learn one new thing from each practice session.

Conduct Drills

Drills require you to do something over and over so that it becomes smooth and automatic. If I want to learn how to do a new dance step, I have to do the first short sequence a 100 times before I can move on to the next sequence. Drills are especially valuable for learning anything that requires physical coordination. The idea is to practice so much that the movements become automatic and you don't have to think about them anymore.

Drills are also useful for rote memorization. Practice over and over until you remember it.

Find a Mentor

Everyone can use a mentor. Find someone you admire or who has the skill sets you want. Perhaps they are an official mentor in your organization. Perhaps they are not so official, simply someone you can ask questions or get guidance from.

Perhaps your mentor will come from an unusual place. My nephew, Victor, showed me this. Victor said he wanted to be like the actor Vin Diesel's characters in the *Fast and Furious* and *Riddick* movies. I use movies all the time for teaching and coaching purposes, but never thought of movie characters as mentors or role models. I studied all the *Fast and Furious* and *Riddick* movies. It turned out Vin Diesel's characters were great mentor-models for Victor. They were strong, kind, value-driven, big, and tough-looking. I found out that a mentor can be anyone and hail from anywhere. Thank you, Victor.

Sometimes, we need a mentor to show us the way or point us in the right direction. Sometimes, mentors help us learn new skills. Or, challenge us. Look for them and observe. Emulate what they do.

Review: Practice

Tools	Things to think about
Practice deliberate practice	What skill, knowledge, or ability have you acquired through deliberate practice? What would you like to learn that would benefit from deliberate practice?
Conduct drills	When have you used drills to learn something?
Find a mentor	Identify three persons you admire who could serve as role models for you.

Don't Be Afraid to Write a Shitty First Draft

Almost all good writing begins with terrible first efforts. You need to start somewhere. Start by getting something—anything—down on paper. What I've learned to do when I sit down to work on a shitty first draft is to quiet the voices in my head.

—Anne Lamott, *Bird by Bird*

I hear people say they would like to write a book, but they haven't yet, the book is all in their head. Sorry, folks, nobody can read the book in your head but you. Eventually you will have to sit down and write. Every road to mastery begins with its own version of the poopy first draft. I remember a client who wanted to write romance novels but was paralyzed because she couldn't get the first page perfect. She didn't understand that the first attempt at anything is rarely perfect. We need to have the courage to sit down and do the work, have the courage to produce that poopy first draft, and have the faith to know that eventually it will get better.

A long time ago, I briefly dated a man who was a ballroom dancer, and he wanted to teach me how to dance—in public. After trying to get me to loosen up, he said, "You're too scared of making mistakes, too scared of what people will think. Don't be afraid to look like a fool." After a few more margaritas, I wasn't afraid to look like a fool. And, I learned a few steps. Now, I don't necessarily advocate drinking margaritas to get you through the fear of looking or sounding stupid, foolish, or silly, but you get my point. Just do it and keep doing it, and eventually, you will have accomplished something of merit.

Go to the Keyboard

Get started. Do it. When I was writing my first book, I would, no matter what, sit down in front of my computer from 8:30 a.m. to 10:30 a.m. every weekday and type. I blocked out that time. No phone calls, no e-mails, no distractions. Sometimes, I would have no clue what I was going to write. Often I dreaded going to the keyboard. Once in a while, I'd still be in pajamas. I learned two things. The hardest part about writing is getting your butt in the chair and your hands on the keyboard. I now know if I put my hands on the keyboard, the words will appear. It's like going to the gym. Sometimes, the hardest part is just getting there.

To develop mastery, you must get started. Enough said.

Get Back on the Horse

Don't give up too easily. Give yourself enough time to know whether it's the thing you want to do. It's not necessary to know what your passion is initially. Or purpose. I stated earlier that I sometimes wonder if passion or purpose are overrated and possibly a bunch of hullabaloo. Just live. Seek what makes you happy.

If we fall off the horse, code for doing it wrong, get back on the horse and do it again. Each time we fall off the horse, we will learn something that will lead to our eventual success.

Review: Don't Be Afraid to Write a Shitty First Draft

Tools	Things to think about
Go to the keyboard	What project or task are you procrastinating about?
Get back on the horse	What activity are you afraid to start again because you fell off the horse and are nervous about getting back on?

Learn New Stuff

Learning new stuff in your journey for mastery can be done in different ways. If we are lucky, continuing to hone our craft or skill or whatever it is we what to be an expert at is a lifelong journey. (I also believe learning will keep us young.)

Frost the Cake

With mastery comes the details, the frosting, the icing on the cake. A good cake is pretty good, but with good frosting, the cake is great. Watch for the details in your craft. I typically suck at details. I am more strategic, more of a big-picture person. Some colleagues call me the "Concept Girl." Once I have proof of concept for my idea, I want to move on. Sometimes, this results in an unfinished, raggedy result. I designed my gazebo garden. It looked fine, but it seemed unfinished. The details were raggedy and messy. I spent last summer tending to the details, and the results were masterful. The gazebo garden is no longer fine. It is stunning.

The details, the frosting, will make a difference.

Make New Cakes

If your thing is welding, learn a new way to weld. If you work with wood, learn to work with engineered wood. If you write fiction, try poetry or reporting. Each time we learn something new about our craft—bake a new kind of cake—it impacts our mastery of that craft. Linda came to me because she was bored at her job. She was considered an expert analyst. She was also an expert at making quilts, though she made only blue quilts. Her blue quilts were technically perfect but seemed lifeless. Boring. She took a quilting class called Color Challenge. Now her blue quilts sizzle with life, with bits of yellow and orange and sometimes red. She did something similar at work. She developed a new analysis process (made a new cake) and began to enjoy her job more because she'd allowed herself to be more creative, more experimental.

Observe How Other People Make Cakes

There is always something to learn from other experts. Find someone whose work or art or technique or style you respect or admire. Observe them in action. I watched a video of world-famous chef, Jacques Pepin, fry an egg. His detail was extraordinary. He described how to fry an egg slowly to keep it tender, how to plate it, decorate it, and lovingly taste it. I never looked at an egg same after that. I am now studying how to boil an egg.

Seek out the experts in your field or area of interest. You may be surprised at how inspired you might be.

Enter a Cake Contest

There is nothing like a contest to polish or practice your skills. If you look, you will find all manner of contests related to what you do. Check out the contests at your local fair. Explore professional associations related to your topic of interest. Then, explore the special interest clubs near you. A local lab here hosts a robot contest. Writing magazines host writing contests. How about a marathon?

Review: Learn New Stuff

Tools	Things to think about
Frost the cake	Describe how you could pay more attention to the details in your area of expertise or interest.
Make new cakes	What is something new that you might learn about your area of expertise or interest?
Observe how other people make cakes	Identify three or four experts that you could observe.
Enter a cake contest	Identify a contest you could consider entering.

Unlearn Old Stuff

The most beautiful form of mastery is the art of letting go.
—Claudia Gray

Sometimes what we already know or do keeps us from learning new things. Sometimes it is a tradition or "we've always done it that way." Sometimes it's a best practice. Business loves best practice because it provides a tried-and-true solution, but it also sometimes suffocates innovation and creativity. Sometimes a belief in our heads tells us that a certain thing has to be done in a certain way. Sometimes we have simply learned bad or sloppy habits. It might be time to unlearn some of that old stuff.

Let Go

I occasionally get clients who are brilliant engineers, scientists, or other technical experts who have recently been promoted. They come to me because they are struggling with how to handle the promotion, especially if they are now in a managerial or leadership position. Usually, the issue is "what got you here, won't get you there." Typically, these clients have to consider leaving the old way behind. That's code for learning a new way. The colonel I mentioned in Chapter 1 had to let go of his brusque military style to succeed in the civilian talent management field. His military style would still be there if he needed it, but he had to let go of it to move forward.

As we continue to master our craft, we need to seek new ways to master it. To do this, we sometimes have to let go of the rules. As Yoda said to Luke Skywalker, "You must unlearn what you have learned."

Special note for business leaders: Don't expect your brilliant engineering, scientific, or other technical experts to automatically become brilliant managers or leaders without teaching them how to be managers or leaders. Provide them the training, mentors, and resources to learn how.

Refresh

We are never too good to sit through another refresher class and go back to basics. The basics are usually the foundation of our craft. If we want to refine or learn something new about that craft, go back to the beginning. I have a mechanic friend who is always revisiting how motors work. He talks about "elegant solutions for motors," which he says are to be discovered in the "basics of motorology."

The basics are often underestimated or dismissed by folks who call themselves experts. Real experts value the basics.

Everything emanates from the basics, from your base. If you don't have a strong base, I'm sorry, but you are always going to be coming back to it, trying to reattain.

—Bill Goldberg

Review: Unlearn Old Stuff

Tools	Things to think about
Let go	Describe what you might have to let go to achieve something new either in your work or an area you are interested in.
Refresh	What are the basics of your craft or area of expertise? Describe how you could go back to basics.

Teach Others

Creating a clear and engaging video explanation of a complex concept is a great way to demonstrate mastery and to help others understand and love the subject too.

—Sal Khan

When I was a kid, I read a story about a boy who was determined to be a spelling bee champion. He asked his friend to help him practice. The friend had the word book and helped the boy spell and pronounce the words every day for an entire summer. The friend studied how to conduct a spelling bee and what rituals were expected. They role-played spelling bees. The friend studied the definitions of words and taught them to the boy. The friend worked tirelessly to teach the boy how to win the spelling bee. Of course, you know the ending. The friend, not the boy, won the spelling bee.

If we want to learn something well, teach it to others. There is research to support this, but let's just say something happens in our brain when we teach others. We understand the skill or topic from a new perspective, which deepens our own expertise. The wonderful thing is that you don't have to be an official teacher to teach. There are many opportunities. Volunteering and creating a how-to are two of them.

Volunteer

Consider teaching as a volunteer. I have a client whose career field is talent management. She volunteers as an instructor at a church to teach others how to write impactful resumes in a digital world, such as online resumes or video resumes. She is trying to learn how to manage talent through the Internet. She is also enjoying it. An engineer friend volunteers as a group leader for teens. He is enjoying the work while building his leadership skills. Notice both people are enjoying themselves. Only volunteer if you want to and enjoy it.

A side benefit of volunteering is its usefulness in a resume. I think a person's volunteer work is the most interesting part of a resume. Employers are looking at this aspect more and more.

Create a How-To

Where do you go when the cucumber leaves fall off? How about when the icemaker malfunctions? Or, how about when you want to boil that egg? You go to the Internet. You type in "how to" and a plethora of how-to videos, e-books, blogs, and websites pop up to tell you how. Some are slick, polished, and professional looking. Some are simple, almost primitive. On YouTube, I like the simple ones: the gardeners who have perfected how to make dirt or the home cooks who have perfected how to make brown rice. I love them.

Have you mastered some skill? If yes, share it. Someone out there in the world wants to know how you did it. So, create something to show them how you did it. Yes, we're interested. This has a triple whammy effect. First, you are sharing your gifts. Second, you are doing the brain thing and deepening your understanding of the subject, and third, you will probably be providing a needed service.

Review: Teach Others

Tools	Things to think about
Volunteer	Describe a skill you have that you would like to practice, either at work or home. Where could you volunteer for one to two hours a month or week to teach this skill? Would you enjoy teaching this skill as a volunteer?
Create a how-to	What skill have you mastered? Describe a how-to you could create to share your skill with others.

Diversify

Once you have mastered the craft, you can use it for whatever purpose you choose.

—Hassan Fathy

Remember the engineer who learned how to weld? Metal Man? Well, he started welding presents for his family. The gifts consisted of whirligigs that moved in the wind, unusual kitchen items, and quirky business card holders. They were so popular that people asked to buy them. Metal Man saw another dimension for his welding business—decorative, whimsical objects. He became particularly interested in how whirligigs moved, and then saw yet another dimension to welding. Art. He now spends his weekends creating metal sculptures that move in the wind. He calls it kinetic sculpture. Metal Man still welds for industrial purposes, but he realized he didn't have to choose just one thing. He now has a metal furniture line, teaches welding, consults on welding projects, and is working on a book.

Branch Out

To branch out means to do something new and different with your existing skills. This allows you to master your craft or skill in a new way and possibly add a fun element. I've had clients who wanted to change careers mostly because they were bored. They were often extremely good at or even experts in their field. One electrical engineer client branched out and began to research how to generate electricity from garbage. He's not bored anymore.

Branching out could mean adding a new dimension to your existing skill like Metal Man and my electrical engineer client did. Branching out could also mean partnering your existing skill with something totally unrelated. My friend George builds houses. He is known for building houses that function according to how we live. He likes to cook and is now going to cooking school. His dream is to specialize in designing and building kitchens for the future.

Create a Portfolio

Creating a portfolio started with folks who retired and still wanted to work. I've heard it referred to as an executive portfolio. A portfolio in this case is just a fancy word for resume. Back to the retirees. They tend to have three to four areas of expertise in their portfolio: the career they retired from, an unrelated skill they are good at, some type of consulting, and often, volunteer work. Think of it as a collection of skills. The mastery aspect is not necessarily expertise in one skill. The mastery is creating the collection.

Nowadays, the portfolio approach is used by anyone who wants to highlight that they are competent at many things. Sometimes it is a collection of part-time, freelance, volunteer, or seasonal jobs. The jobs may or may not be related. Often when we list these types of jobs on a resume, employers don't view it favorably. Take that same resume, call it a portfolio, and those same employers will like the term *portfolio* and hire you.

Two summers ago, I needed to hire a housekeeper to clean and stage my mom's house in Homer, Alaska. We had converted the house into a bed-and-breakfast and I needed to find someone to take care of the house for me (I live in Edgewood, New Mexico). Ten minutes prior to her interview time, Amanda walked up the driveway as she stared at her smartphone. Her truck had broken down, so she walked to our house and used her phone GPS for directions. She had started out early so she wouldn't be late. As she walked through the door, she noticed it was broken. "I can fix that," she said. "I'm a handyman on the side." She had no resume. She also noticed the little flower garden out front. "Do you need someone to take care of the flowers?" She was a gardener too. We talked, and I learned that she'd recently arrived in Alaska with very little money to start a new chapter in her life. She had no references. But she had a collection—a portfolio—of skills I needed: dependability, good decision making, creativity, and flexibility. I hired her as the house manager on the spot. After that, I did everything I could to keep her happy, and she did a glorious job as house manager. Thank you, Amanda.

A portfolio can have several advantages. It can offer different skill sets to different employers. It can offer you more control over your career. It can diversify your job offerings so you're not putting all your eggs into one basket. It can provide flexibility. It can alleviate boredom. The portfolio approach is not for everyone. There are disadvantages. Often there are no benefits, and there is uncertainty, so networking or marketing yourself is extra important.

Sometimes the portfolio approach relates to the gig economy, fueled by gig workers. This involves part-time workers, freelancers, temporary or seasonal workers, specialty workers, or independent contractors. The *resume* becomes a collection of part-time or temporary jobs originally referred to as gigs. In the beginning, the gig economy usually involved young people, but that is not the case anymore.

Review: Diversify

Tools	Things to think about
Branch out	What do you do in the workplace? What could you do to add a new element to your work, especially an element that you would enjoy?
Create a portfolio	Describe your portfolio here.

Be Ready: The Universe Will Test You

You are always a student, never a master. You have to keep moving forward.

—Conrad Hall

Once you believe you are there—the master—beware the universal thumping. There will always be someone better or faster or smarter or higher-ranking or richer or thinner or funnier than you. Just when you think "I am *it*," don't! Someone will appear in this universe to thump you down. Ishmael, in Herman Melville's *Moby-Dick,* describes it well:

> What of it, if some old hunks of a sea-captain orders me to get a broom and sweep down the decks? What does that indignity amount to weighed, I mean, in the scales of the New Testament? Do you think the archangel Gabriel thinks anything the less of me, because I promptly and respectfully obey that old hunks in that particular instance? Who ain't a slave? Tell me that. Well, then, however the old sea-captains may order me about—however they may thump and punch me about, I have the satisfaction of knowing that it is all right; that everybody else is one way or other served in much the same way—either in a physical or metaphysical point of view, that is; and so the universal thump is passed round, and all hands should rub each other's shoulder blades, and be content.

Continue to learn and master your craft. Regardless how good we become, no matter what stature we achieve, we all go poo-poo. We are all the same in the eyes of the universe. And, there will always be the universal thump to remind us. Continue learning and honing your craft, whatever form it takes.

Perhaps you still haven't found a craft to master. That's OK. Master the journey. Master the search. Perhaps master living a happy life.

When you become an expert, recognize the expert in others. Revel in their skill. Tell them. Learn from them.

When the universe does thump you, have faith in yourself. "It's all right," as Ishmael says. "The universal thump is passed around, and all hands should rub each other's shoulder blades, and be content."

CHAPTER 4

Grow Your Pennies

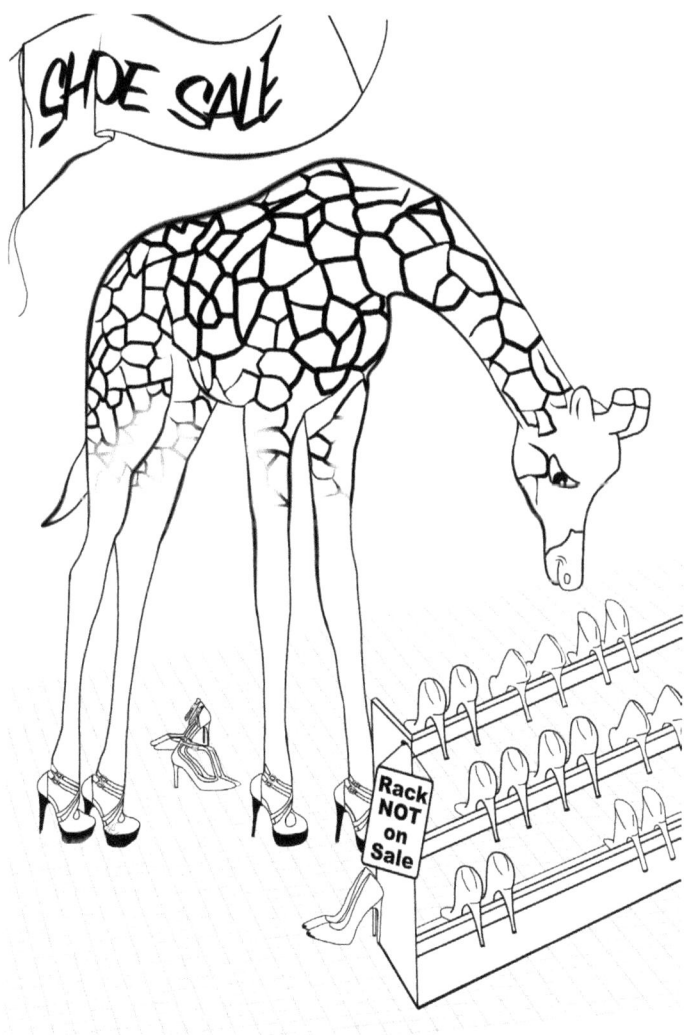

If you expect your money to take care of you, you must take care of your money.

—Suze Orman

So many of my clients have money issues. Some live on the edge between having just enough and flat out having no money at all. Some work at well-paying jobs while struggling to support a large house, maintain three cars, and pay for child care or private schools. They are living on the edge because they are living beyond their means. Other clients are unhappy at their jobs but get paid so well they won't leave. They are wearing golden handcuffs. Some clients are undergoing financial stress as they change careers or begin to reinvent themselves. They are rethinking how they view money or how they view happiness. In my experience, money almost always plays a significant role in the lives of my career-coaching clients.

My clients almost always have to address money before they can address career change. And, they cannot address happiness or purpose or passion if they can't pay the bills or provide for their family. Our coaching plans for career change always bring money into the conversation.

I am no finance expert, but I can share with you what I've learned from my own as well as my clients' experiences managing financial matters. Here is my short list of favorite people and places to go to read or research financial advice:

- Warren Buffet, investor billionaire and philanthropist, famous for investment strategy. I like that he seems to live simply even though he is a billionaire.
- Suze Orman, financial advisor who has many written books and hosted podcasts and her own television show. I like that I can understand what she is saying and can apply what she says to my own situation.
- The Motley Fool web page (www.fool.com), published by a private financial and investing advice company. I like their easy-to-understand advice and information.

Grow Your Pennies: What Does It Mean?

A nickel ain't worth a dime anymore.

—**Yogi Berra**

Today's money works differently for us than it did twenty years ago. There was a time when a person could save money in a classic savings account and possibly even earn a bit of interest. Some folks bought savings bonds or treasury bonds. Other folks had piggy banks. When I was young, my mom saved money in white envelopes. For middle-class, working America, the main premise was to save money. If interest could be earned at the same time, so much the better. For a moment in time, savings accounts and other savings programs paid good interest. But, the basic tenet was to save. That is not the case anymore. Interest paid on savings is no longer what it used to be. Plus, the value of your savings is not what it used to be. With inflation, recession, and all manner of economic ups and downs, the actual value of the money can change. The adage "a penny saved is a penny earned" has changed.

Consider a new adage, "A penny invested is two pennies earned." It is time to invest. There are many ways to invest. It is not solely about stocks and bonds or fancy annuities. It's also about what we buy and don't buy, the financial decisions we make, and even our outlook on life.

Grow Your Pennies: Why?

The best thing money can buy is financial freedom.

—Rob Berger

The first reason to grow your pennies, to invest, is to obtain financial security. The test for this is to ask, "How long can I pay the bills if I lose my job?" One month? Six months? No months? Then ask, "What's at stake?" Who depends on you? Is it just you? If yes, maybe it's OK to be penniless or homeless and seeking your fortune. Is it you, your children, elderly parents, and a dog? The stakes just got higher. It's time to grow your money.

With sound investing and financial decision making, the ultimate result is financial freedom. This, in turn, will allow us to change careers, pursue other interests, seek passion and purpose, and look ahead confidently to retirement.

Start an Emergency Fund

It may take you months or even a few years to build up adequate emergency savings fund. That's okay.

—**Suze Orman**

As with any garden project, before we start growing anything, we need to prepare the soil. In this case, the soil is an emergency fund. In my garden, the dirt is the most important piece to the successful growth of anything. It is the foundation to build upon. In personal finance, an emergency fund serves as the foundation. Unless we are so wealthy that large, unexpected expenses won't affect us, an emergency fund should be our first and highest priority. Often called the rainy-day fund, the emergency fund is supposed to be there to cover unexpected expenses, such as car or home repairs or medical bills. It can also be there to help cover lost income.

My client Amy wanted to change careers. It would mean a decrease in pay, which she was willing to do. She had no savings and no emergency fund. She did have a mortgage and a car loan. The new job would pay her bills, but just barely. One mistake, one binge, one splurge, one unplanned expense would mean trouble. We talked about an emergency fund and financially preparing her to take on the lesser-paying job in the new career field.

"I want to totally commit to the new job," she said. "I want to *have* to succeed at it." She was excited but afraid her opportunity would disappear. She wanted to jump immediately. And, she did! She jumped and did well. For a while.

I got a call from Amy about six months later. She had paid a large car repair bill instead of paying the electric bill. "They turned off my electricity. I haven't paid them in three months. Now I have to pay for the three months plus a reinstallation fee," she said. She was broke and sounded desperate. "I didn't think they'd turn off the electricity. I wish I'd set up that emergency fund."

I referred her to a financial coach. It turned out that Amy was able to get a bailout. She procured a short-term loan for the electric bill, though she had no electricity for two days. Then, the first thing she did with her financial coach was to plan how to start an emergency fund. She also took on a weekend job to help pay the bills until she was more established in her new career field.

We never want to be in a situation where we need a bailout. We need to be able to handle whatever happens, no matter how bad it gets.

Determine How Much

How much money should we have in our emergency fund? There are a lot of rules about this. Some folks say three to six months' worth of our salary. Or whatever it takes to pay our bills. Others say it should be 10 percent of our salary. My suggestion is that you ignore the rules. Start an emergency fund and do the best you can.

How much also depends on who depends on you. If you are supporting a family, the consequences are different if you can't pay the rent or your house is taken back by the bank. The amount also depends on where you are financially right now. The amount you determine you need may be totally unrealistic. It may be that saving pennies in a jar is all that is possible. That's OK. How much is up to you and what is possible for you. Do your best, regardless how small. Just get started.

Manage It

Back to the jar. When I was an undergrad, I bought a quart mason jar at a flea market. It was painted all artsy with a log cabin motif and labeled "tax shelter." I used it to hold loose change. When full, it was worth about $65. Several times a year I harvested that $65. It was my first emergency fund management system. I bought many packages of ramen noodles with that emergency fund. My husband did the same with a beer stein.

Beyond jars and beer steins, there are two questions to ask when it comes to how to manage an emergency fund. First, where will you put it?

Second, will the money be readily available when an emergency occurs? Here are some possibilities to consider:

- A savings account: Look for one with a higher-than-average interest rate and no monthly fees or balance requirements. It should be an account dedicated to your emergency fund. You can make withdrawals anytime.
- A money market account: They sometimes offer higher interest rates than a regular savings account. You can withdraw anytime with most; however, double-check to make sure there isn't a penalty for withdrawals. Also, look for check-writing privileges and online or mobile banking.
- A certificate of deposit (CD): They are offered for a fixed rate of return for a specific period, such as years. Early withdrawals usually incur a penalty, but in an emergency, the penalty may be moot.
- Yes, go ahead and find a jar or a beer stein. It doesn't matter. I know a lady who uses an old teapot.

Fund It

We have our management system (account or jar), and now we need to fund it. This means put money into it. If possible, one way to do this is to put 1 to 10 percent of your salary into the emergency fund. This is especially easy if your company offers automatic deposits to your bank accounts. Then, sit tight. Don't peek. It's not there. It's only there for an emergency. Hands off.

If you can't start an emergency fund through a company salary, you will have to summon up the discipline and patience to do it on your own. Start by figuring out where you will find the money. Do you even know what you spend your money on?

Identify your critical expenses. These are expenses you have to pay for. They are your needs, such as a car payment, rent or a mortgage payment, utilities, groceries, Internet, smartphone, school, or school loans. These are usually recurring expenses we pay every month. Be sure to include critical expenses that occur once or twice a year, such as property taxes.

Now identify all your other monthly expenses. These are usually your wants, such as clothing, entertainment, furnishings, house remodeling, or in my case, stuff for the garden.

Here is where the lines between need and want can blur. Sometimes what seems like a want can be a need. I had a neighbor once who was on welfare. The state paid for her rent, and she had food stamps for groceries. Yet she had a fancy subscription for a cable TV service. She explained the cable TV seemed luxurious, but it actually was an inexpensive way to entertain her five children at home. They had movie nights and all types of activities that involved television shows or movies. One kid was learning to cook by watching the Food Channel. What seemed frivolous, the cable TV subscription, had become a need.

Smartphones and the Internet may seem like a want. However, the reality of COVID-19 has proven to us that we live in a digital world. I can work from home and go to school because of the Internet. Students go to school online. Corporations meet online. Many businesses are booming online. There is online banking, shopping, chatting, advice-getting, and information-seeking. For me, a smartphone and Internet are a need. I also see a smartphone as critical for children and teens, so they can call for help in an emergency.

Then there is the fun factor or the enjoyment factor. I think I read this in one of Suze Orman's books. The enjoyment factor involves an expense that enhances your quality of life so much that you should not delete it. Ever. Jenny, my client for two years, likes to travel with her husband. They get supreme pleasure in going to new places and revisiting old favorite places. They research the history, visit the landmarks, attempt to meet the local folks, and enjoy local foods. At home, they try to re-create the recipes, make scrapbooks, or watch documentaries of places they visited or want to visit. They attend lectures and travel clubs. If they can travel, they are happy to scrimp on new clothes, nice cars, a fancy place to live, or expensive forms of entertainment. Then, Jenny decided she wanted to go back to school full-time to become a dentist. She and her husband worked together on creating a plan for this and were sad at first because they thought they'd have to give up traveling. My advice is, "Give up everything else. Do not give up what you love."

Now that we know where and what we spend our money on, find one expense to reduce or delete. It doesn't matter how small. If it's only a dollar, it's a very important dollar. It's your first step. Use the dollar to start your emergency fund. Put that money in your account (or jar) and forget about it. Then congratulate yourself. You are on your way.

Warning: Don't let the pundits and financial gurus scare you or intimidate you. Just get started in a way that works for you.

Identify What Is an Emergency

Let's be clear. An emergency fund is not for vacations, or a way to make money for holiday shopping. It has one purpose only: to pay for emergencies. Be sure you understand what you consider to be an emergency. This will differ for each person.

Special note for businesses: Find a way to establish an emergency fund. At a minimum, know what expenses you can delete if an emergency happens.

Special note for startups and entrepreneurs: Money is often a different story. Often, every penny is put toward the business. Financially survive any way you can as long as it is ethical, moral, and legal. You can have ramen noodles every night.

Review: Start an Emergency Fund

Tools	Things to think about
Determine how much	In a perfect world, how much money do you think should be in your emergency fund? What is a realistic goal for you to have in your emergency fund after one year?
Manage it	How will you manage your emergency fund?
Fund it	What are your critical expenses (your needs)? What are your other expenses (your wants)? What expense involves an enjoyment factor? What is one expense you could consider deleting?
Identify what is an emergency	What situations and expenses would you classify as an emergency? Do you have the ability and patience to leave the money in the emergency fund to be used only for emergencies?

Invest

How many millionaires do you know who have become wealthy by investing in savings accounts? I rest my case.

—Robert G. Allen

To grow our pennies in today's world, we will usually have to invest those pennies. What is an investment? According to Merriam-Webster dictionary, an investment is "the outlay of money usually for income or profit." An article in *The Simple Dollar* says an investment is anything you put money into with the expectation that you will *earn* money as a result.

Stocks and bonds are investments because the expectation is that owning them will earn us money. College tuition is an investment because the expectation is that we will earn more money in our career than the cost of college. Other things sound like investments but are not.

For example, you might purchase a more expensive car, such as a Volvo, because it is known to last many, many years and has an excellent safety record. (No, I don't own a Volvo. I own an old Jeep Wrangler.) The Volvo may be a good financial decision, but it is not an investment. However, if you buy a supercar or a collectible car that gains value with time, that would be an investment because you could gain a profit if you sold it.

An investment makes you money. Using the old garden analogy, it grows your pennies. As with any garden, there is an element of risk. In my actual garden, the risk includes hail, early or late frosts, grasshoppers, and fuzzy critters. For investments, the risk involves your tolerance for risk, your ability to be patient, and the specific investment you select.

Be Patient

"The stock market is designed to transfer money from the active to the patient," says investment expert Warren Buffett. He also says you don't need to be particularly intelligent to be a successful investor. He advocates patience and the temperament to control the urges that get other people into trouble when investing. Thus, the first guideline for investing: be patient. Your patience may be needed several times. If you have no money, you'll need to be patient and save enough money to make even a tiny investment (after you have started your emergency fund).

Perhaps it's not possible or it's unrealistic right now for you to save any money for investing. If that's the case, go direct to the section *Learn About Investing*.

If you have money you can invest, you will need to be patient while you select the best investment for you. After investing, you will need to be patient and sit tight while that investment grows. Then the toughest patience test comes. Market turbulence *will* happen says Matthew Frankel and Charlie Munger of The Motley Fool. It's not an *if*, but a *when*. We must be patient and mentally tough enough not to panic during downward moves.

Your investment will go up and down. Unless you are interested in playing the market, hunker down and wait. Unless you selected something that is very high risk and volatile, your investment will probably survive any turbulence. My investments plummeted when the coronavirus pandemic hit the United States full force in March 2020. I felt the panicky, sinking feeling, but sat tight. Six months later, the investments rebounded and actually increased in value.

It's patience. Some call it a money mindset. Or temperament. Some say it's how we learn about money. Sandra came to me freshly retired after spending 20 years in the Army as an officer. She grew up in a family of money managers. Her father was an accountant, and her mother a bookkeeper. Sandra had begun investing the day she was born because her parents started her out. She grew up learning the art of managing money and investing and saw it as a source of freedom.

When Sandra retired from the Army, she was 43 years old and had a healthy Army retirement pay and a large investment portfolio that netted her good dividends. She also had an emergency fund and belonged to an investment club. She came to me because she wanted help figuring out what her next career should be. She has been my only client who could do anything she wanted without having to develop a financial plan to do it. Her financial security gave her that freedom.

Think Like an Owner

The most important investment you can make is in yourself.
—**Warren Buffet**

Even if you have only one measly share in a company, it means you are part owner of that company. This is the second guideline for investing. Think like an owner. Buy into a company because you want to own it, not because you want to make money. Here are some tips from Warren Buffet:

- Never invest in a business you cannot understand. Risk comes from not knowing what you're doing.
- If you don't feel comfortable making a rough estimate of the asset's future earnings, just forget it and move on.
- Buy companies with strong histories of profitability and with a dominant business franchise.

According to The Motley Fool, there's a reason you won't find a bunch of biotech or high-growth technology companies in Warren Buffett's portfolio. He doesn't understand them, so he doesn't invest in them. Not only should you understand the businesses you invest in, but stick to companies with established track records of profitability, products consumers love, and that are among the top companies in their industries.

You could also do the opposite—think like a customer. What products do you use every day, year after year? I use Mary Kay, Microsoft, my Jeep, and Miracle Grow garden soil. Guess what I am or should be invested in? The idea is to love what you are invested in. Be proud of it.

Go for quality. It's better to have a partial interest in the crown jewels than to own all of a rhinestone.

Ignore market noise. According to Warren Buffett, the worst mistake an investor can make is to pay too much attention to commentators on TV, political drama, or market rumors. "Most people get interested in stocks when everyone else is. The time to get interested is when no one else is." You can't buy what is trendy or popular in the moment and do well. When it comes to politics, American business will do just fine over the long run, no matter who is in the White House.

Then there is the gold controversy. Some experts say buy gold. Harry Browne, author of *The Economic Time Bomb*, says gold is the best investment to protect against inflation.

Others say the opposite. Matthew Frankel of The Motley Fool says this about gold: "I have no views as to where it [gold] will be, but the one thing I can tell you is, it won't do anything between now and then except look at you." If you can afford to buy gold, please do some research first so you can *understand* gold. Then, get real gold, not stocks in gold mines or gold mining companies. For most of us, gold is not an issue because we can't afford it, but it is still good to be informed. Perhaps the day will come when we can afford it.

And then there are the investing advisors, brokers, and salespeople. When investing geniuses David and Tom Gardner have a stock tip, it can pay to listen. After all, the newsletter they have run for over a decade, *Motley Fool Stock Advisor*, has consistently provided sound advice. It doesn't cost anything to listen. However, be cautious with expert advice and recommendations when it comes to where you can put or spend your money. This is especially true if you have a system that is working for you.

Learn About Investing

Sometimes we aren't ready to invest because we either don't have the money or don't know what to do. Sit tight. Remember patience. You can begin your investment journey by learning about investing.

Listen to the news. Watch the how the stock market goes up and down according to what's happening in the world. Perhaps select a specific stock and follow it. Notice how companies start up, boom, split up, diversify, or go out of business.

Develop the temperament, the money mindset. This means developing patience. Learn how to wait it out, sit tight. Developing patience will be different for everyone. Develop your own way and how you will decide to invest when opportunity has struck. Remember, we will need patience to allow our money to grow, and we will need patience to weather the storms. Once, on the way home, I was caught in a big thunderstorm. I was anxious to get home, but hail was pummeling my windshield, and the lightning and thunder were right on top of me. I pulled over to a safe place and sat tight and waited out the storm. Do the same with your investments.

Experiment. Select a stock and follow it. Research its past performance. Pretend you've invested your life savings in it. Watch what happens at different checkpoints: at a month, then three months, six months, a year. Take notes at each checkpoint. What happens to your pretend investment? Between checkpoints, learn everything you can about your stock. Watch how world events affect it, or don't.

Review: Invest

Tools	Things to think about
Be patient (develop the temperament for investing)	Describe your money mindset. • What do you believe about money? Can you save for tomorrow or do you live for today? • What do you believe about debt? • What do you believe about spending money? • What were you taught about money as a child? Describe your level of patience. • What do you think about money for the future? • Describe something that took you a long time to accomplish. If you won $5 million in the lottery today, how would you spend it?
Think like an owner	What companies would you like to own? What products do you use?
Learn about investing	What are some ways you can learn about investing?

Rethink the House Myth

A man builds a fine house; and now he has a master, and a task for life; he is to furnish, watch, show it, and keep it in repair, the rest of his days.

—Ralph Waldo Emerson

Home is where the heart is. There's no place like home. Home, sweet home. The very sound of the word *home* evokes a tender yet primal quality that many yearn for. And, it sells houses because we want to fill that yearning. We want home. We love home. We make a good investment when we buy a home. *And we are deluded.* We buy a house, not a home. A house is not a home until it is filled with people who live there, who create memories there, and who experience life there. A house is not an investment. A house is a shelter, a place to feel safe and do all that memory-creation stuff. It is not an investment.

With an investment, we can get our money back when needed. We can make a profit. When we buy a house, we are usually buying for that shelter, status, enjoyment, pride, and the famous memory-making. For most of us, buying a house will be the biggest expense we take on. But that is OK, we are told. Your house is an investment. *We are deluded again.* How many people truly own their house? In reality, the bank owns it. If you miss your house payments, the bank will take away your house. So, you don't really own it.

Houses are the number one issue with my clients. They are often young clients who want to change careers or travel but are tied down by a house payment that often takes 40 to 50 percent of their salary. They haven't *owned* the house long enough to sell it and make a profit. Sometimes they owe more on the house than the house is worth. Or, the clients are older and want to retire and start a new chapter in their lives. They still have a house payment that eats up a large chunk of their income. They are often reluctant to sell their house for a myriad of reasons: visiting children and grandchildren, the community, poor real estate market, or those memories.

Determine What Your House Really Is

A house is a shelter, not an investment. It is a place to live. If you sell your house, you still need a place to live. You might make a profit and use that profit to buy a bigger house. If you sell your house, make a profit, and downsize to a smaller house, that could be an investment. Houses do increase in value, but that doesn't make it an investment. It's not an investment just because it appreciates. The real reason a house appreciates over 40 years is probably just inflation. That's not to say real estate values cannot appreciate dramatically. They can and do, but mostly in special locations such as San Francisco or Tokyo.

A true investment typically has little or no carrying costs. The carrying costs are the purchase price, maintenance costs, taxes, and any other costs associated with ownership. Consider the carrying costs for a house. First, there are the costs just to get into the house, such as the cost of buying the house, realtor fees, possible title searches, and property inspections. After the house is purchased, there are the ongoing carrying costs to maintain and operate the property. There are property taxes, property insurance, private mortgage insurance, maintenance and repairs, and possibly, homeowner's association fees. Don't forget any optional costs such as remodeling or upgrading and landscaping. I've heard people say that owning a house is the American dream. I've heard others say it is a money pit.

Now consider the carrying costs for a typical investment. The typical investment has a broker or transaction fee. There might be a fee or penalty for early withdrawal or borrowing on the investment.

Investments are liquid. We can buy, sell, and convert to cash relatively easily. Of course, you can sell your house anytime, but it usually takes time. It also usually takes a real estate agent, but that is changing rapidly. There are already online applications for buying and selling houses and the paperwork process is becoming easier for people to buy and sell houses without a realtor. If we're lucky, our house sells fast at a good price, and we make a profit. Then we find a new place to live, which can be an arduous process for many people. If you never plan to sell your house, it can't be an investment because you will never make a profit on it. If your heirs sell the house, they should make a profit.

Thinking of your house as an investment can also lead to what is called equity stripping. This involves getting a second mortgage, which is basically using your house as collateral for a loan.

Determine what your house really is. Is it a place to make memories or an investment? If you want it to be an investment, "put your money into true investments, like financial assets or real estate that produces rental income," says Ryan Frailich, a certified financial planner. If you want your house to be a home, a safe haven, and a place to make memories, Frailich says to "kick back and enjoy living in your house. That's the real purpose of owning one."

Never feel like you *have* to buy a house. There's social pressure to do so, but it should be behind other priorities in your financial life. Get an emergency fund built. When you can, save at least 10 percent of your income for retirement. Get your student loans under control and have a plan to pay them off. Aim for no credit card debt. Once all of those are done, then consider home ownership, advises *The Simple Dollar*.

Know When to Buy or Not to Buy

To buy a house or not to buy a house, that is a big question. How do we know when the time is right? Here are some ideas to consider:

- Buy—if it makes you happy
- Buy—if it saves you money over the long term compared to the alternatives
- Buy—if you plan to stay there at least five years
- Buy—if someone else is paying the mortgage, such as with rental income or roommates
- Rent—if you're not sure where you'll be living three to five years from now
- Rent—if you can't make a sizable down payment
- Rent—if you can't handle the initial or ongoing carrying costs
- Rent—if you don't really want to own a house

Create Cash Flow

When my mom went to live with my sister, we converted my mom's house into a bed-and-breakfast in the beautiful town of Homer, Alaska. We were open for business only for the summer, and we were booked solid the entire season. We generated enough income to support the house for the entire year. This meant my mom didn't have to pay the bills for the house, and she was pleased that other people were enjoying her home. Granted, we weren't living in the house at the same time, but it gives an idea of how your house can create cash flow. Here are some more ideas:

- Rent your house when you go on vacation.
- Rent a room in your house.
- If you have college-bound kids, buy a house or condo for them near their school. Rent out extra rooms. Keep it for the entire time your kids are in college. Then, sell it.

- Rent out storage space.
- Become an event venue, especially if you have an amazing location.
- Provide day care for children, elders, or pets. Check out local regulations, what skills or certifications you might need, what help you might need, and what you can handle. The demand for high-quality care in these areas is growing, and any of these specialties could become a full-time job. But keeping the scope small may work best. My friend Deb provides day care for one elderly lady. It's quite a serene picture. Deb works from home, usually on a computer. The elderly lady likes giant jigsaw puzzles and listens to audio books through noise-canceling headphones.

When seeking to create cash flow with your house, cover all the bases. Check with your homeowner's insurance. Be sure you are up to this. Check homeowner's association rules and local ordinances. Licenses might be needed.

Review: Rethink the House Myth

Tools	Things to think about
Determine what your house really is	Do you consider your house to be an investment? Why or why not?
Know when to buy or not to buy	If you don't already own a house, when might you be ready to buy one? If you own a house now, when might you sell it?
Create cash flow	What is one way you might be able to create cash flow with your house?

Be Ready: The Universe Will Test You

Life sends you tests, like those of patience, as a gift for your growth.
—Heather Corinne Lang

There will always be something to spend your money on in lieu of saving or investing, even sudden money storms of necessary or unnecessary spending. There will be temptations. There will be a battle between what you need and what you want. There will be emergencies. There will be unexpected expenses. There will be golden opportunities to invest in or spend money on, or so you think. There will be family and friends who borrow money and may or may not repay you. There will be scammers. There will be ups and downs in the stock market.

It is up to us to develop a money mindset that will help us weather the storm and create financial freedom. Can we learn the fine art of delayed gratification? Can we master the skill of saying no, and when to say it and when not to say it? Can we sit tight and patiently wait out a money storm. Can we say yes?

CHAPTER 5

Tenacity

Inspiration leads to invention. Tenacity is the breeding ground for inspiration. There can be no invention in the absence of tenacity.

—Momofuku Ando

Tenacity is an age-old quality that humans have demonstrated through-out time. However, it is a quality that has become overlooked in today's fast-moving, get-it-now, efficiency-based world. Tenacity is the quality of being able to grip something firmly and hold fast. Tenacity gives us the ability to persevere and continue holding on despite difficulties, failure, or opposition. "Tenacity is the number one trait of successful entrepreneurs. They have to deal with failure," writes Joe Robinson in an article in *Entrepreneur* magazine (January 2014).

Tenacity or Persistence?

To succeed in life in today's world, you must have the will and tenacity to finish the job.

—Chin-Ning Chu

Life is not always pretty. Our ability to persevere, to get back up when we fall down, to bounce back and continue may be one of the most important skills we can develop. However, this is not tenacity. This is perseverance. Tenacity is when you keep trying, but if it doesn't work out, you try different approaches. I'll agree they're similar in meaning. Both tenacious and persistent persons possess a will that refuses to submit. However, it's the manner in which they refuse that's entirely different, with tenacity being decidedly more effective at helping us achieve success.

A persistent person will try something again and again in the hopes that it will eventually work. Regardless of how flawed the method, they never amend or vary their approach. They're content to think that if they continue to try, sooner or later things will pay off. Persistence is admirable in its unrelenting approach and often signifies a hard worker. Pete Boyle of have-a-word.com says persistence is the hallmark of a freelancer who chooses to work harder, not smarter. The ability to try again and again and hope it will eventually work is the mark of a hard worker.

Boyle goes on to say that tenacity, on the other hand, is the mark of the strategic thinker. A tenacious person is never content with their methodology. They possess the same indomitable will as their persistent counterpart, but choose to utilize the information and data from their previous attempts to further improve their methodology. Tenacity is more strategic. The tenacious will try again and again, but each time they'll try to improve their method. They are flexible, examining options and possibilities, and gathering the information they need to succeed.

Why Is Tenacity Important?

Life is a course with endless obstacles to hurdle.

—Nelson Mandela

Hard work may not always be the answer. Effort alone is not a measure of success. Our lives are full of challenges. Some are easy, but many, if not most, are difficult. The challenges come by different names: obstacles, adversities, crises, traumatic events, and anything that confronts us or presents us with difficulties. A potential outcome of all these challenges is that we give up, quit, or never get started. We need tenacity.

My client Carolyn is just out of college, and we've been working together for a couple of months. She's angry because she has submitted about 10 job applications (all online due to the COVID-19 pandemic) for positions that suit her skill set, and she's been rejected each time. She feels she's been lied to or tricked by well-meaning parents and teachers who have always told her that she can do and be anything she wants in life. Frankly, these people have unwittingly done her a disservice by implying that whatever she wants is hers to have and that it should come easily. Carolyn has yet to develop true tenacity, not only because she is inexperienced but because she is someone who, in spite of dealing with several disabilities, has always been able to easily accomplish her goals. She figured finding a job would be another easily attained accomplishment.

Carolyn is highly intelligent, creative, and passionate, but on the verge of giving up on her dreams because she has taken the rejections too personally. Up until this point, because things have come easily for her, she has never had to reevaluate her approach or try something different to get what she wants. The acute discouragement she feels and her lack of tenacity are hurting her chances of find a job or career path that will support her long-term goals. During a recent Zoom session, she announced, "I quit. I'm going to go work at McDonald's or just live off my disability check!"

Having tenacity provides a way to see setbacks as short-term obstacles that need to be solved in service of a larger goal. So, I encouraged Carolyn to come up with innovative and creative ways to revamp her resume, to make it stand out. She may even add to her resume a video in which she talks about her experience and her dreams for her future. Tenacity is about having faith in yourself and holding on even if it takes more work than you thought it would.

Fortunately, tenacity can be learned, practiced, and developed. For some of us, this can take time. For others, tenacity is instinctual and already in us, but might be forgotten or repressed. We cannot just wish our way to our goals. We have to take action. We learn from taking step one and then fine-tuning it before we go on to step two. Tenacity is the opposite of wishful thinking, daydreaming, or just hoping it'll get done.

Special note for leaders: Leaders need to model tenacity for their staff by demonstrating and encouraging innovative solutions to overcoming obstacles. Rory Gori says leaders need to encourage tenacity in their staff, seek tenacity in hiring practices, and model tenacity.

A leader should have higher grit and tenacity and be able to endure what the employees can't.

—**Jack Ma**

Know Where You Are Going

If you don't know where you are going, you might wind up someplace else.

—**Yogi Berra**

You may not know exactly *how* you will get there, but if you have some idea of where you want to go before you start, you will be better able to access the energy of tenacity.

I'm a gardener, and one summer, I decided to create a dry stream bed in the ditch by the side of the road by my house. I ordered seven tons (!) of beautiful rocks that were delivered and dumped in a big pile in our driveway. I had a 100 feet of ditch to turn into a dry stream bed. It was completely overwhelming!

I knew what I wanted the dry stream bed to look like, but I had no idea how I was going to transfer seven tons of rocks from my driveway to the ditch. I encountered many obstacles in the process, from not being able to maneuver more than half a wheelbarrow of rocks at a time, to working in 100-degree heat, but I was tenacious in my drive to complete my project because I knew exactly what I wanted. My vision drove me to continuously innovate ways to execute my task and kept me going even when I had no idea how to move forward. By having a clear vision and knowing where you're going, you can overcome obstacles in your path.

Define Your Goal or Task

I could visualize my dry stream bed, but I didn't set milestones, which would have been helpful. I also didn't have a way to evaluate how the job was progressing, which would have made it easier for me to anticipate the problems I might encounter along the way. I should have:

- Created a set of milestones
- Found a way to monitor or evaluate
- Based on monitoring, revised, made course corrections, or created with new options
- Developed a simple contingency plan for obstacles

Know Why You're Doing It

I created the dry stream bed in the ditch because, as an avid gardener, I felt passionately that I did not want an ugly ditch next to my beautiful garden. And, in spite of the challenges I encountered—the weeds that pushed up through my carefully laid rocks, the extreme heat, the intense physical labor—I enjoyed every minute of the work. I love physical activity, I love tackling challenges, I love making my garden beautiful, and I love being one of the crazy lady gardeners in the neighborhood.

What if your boss gives you a tough project you have no interest in doing, but you have to do it to keep your job? In that situation, how do you find the tenacity and fortitude to do it? You don't have an investment in the project itself. Perhaps, because doing it serves your team and your company and ensures your livelihood, you find that you are able to muster the motivation to tackle the project. And, by looking at it as an opportunity to learn something new or partner with somebody who can teach you something, you find that you can access the tenacity to conquer your resistance and move forward.

It is important to know why we are doing things or we won't ever have the tenacity to do them. The *what* doesn't matter. The *why* can be camouflaging an ugly ditch or supporting your family or getting a new car. There must be a why.

Review: Know Where You Are Going

Tools	Things to think about
Define your goal	Describe a project that took you a long time to complete. What were the challenges involved in this project? How did you overcome the challenges? Did you finish the project?
Know why you're doing it	Why did you take on this project?

Get Started

The most difficult thing is the decision to act, the rest is merely tenacity.
—Amelia Earhart

Show Up

Legend has it that the most difficult part of any endeavor is showing up. Getting to the gym is probably the classic example. For many people, the act of getting to the gym is the hardest part about working out.

Showing up is about taking action. Commitment. Now. Not tomorrow. Not next week. Not when everything is perfect. Stop thinking about it. Stop resisting. Get there.

- Go to the gym.
- Go to the class.
- Go to the meeting.
- Go to where the clients are.
- Go to the keyboard.
- Go to the easel.
- Get your butt there.
- Make the commitment.
- Go now.

Some folks advocate preparing and planning and creating goals and objectives before showing up. That's fine, but for me, planning is often just another name for procrastination. If you need to make a plan, do it. I made a plan for my new rock garden, but only after I showed up with a landscaper. I made another plan for a paper I'm writing, but only after I showed up at the library to do a little research. Plans are good and are often needed, but for outliers, plans can sometimes be a form of paralysis. To show up means to go to the place where we need to go to take action, to the place where we take the first step. To go. It's a verb. It's an action. If you are an outlier like me, you will need action to compel more action to keep going. In our house, we often say that "energy breeds energy."

Perhaps, think of showing up as making a commitment in the form of action. We've all heard the old action adages such as "actions speak louder than words," or "vision without action is just a daydream," or "justice is truth in action," or "let's make a call for action," or "heroes take action." I think Pablo Picasso said it best, "Action is the foundational key to all success." So, take action and get there. Show up.

Take the First Step

After you show up, do something. The first step can be tough. People ask me, "What do I do?" I can only speak from what I do. As a writer, I show up at the keyboard and punch the first key and have faith the words will come. Sometimes, the words start slowly, and they are only words, not sentences. Then a word will inspire another word, and another word until I finally have a sentence. Then the energy-breeds-energy philosophy kicks in and I create momentum and the words pour out. I never have writer's block. I get my butt to the keyboard and punch that first key.

Push the first rep. Pick up the first rock. Pull the first weed. Take the first lesson. Make the first call. Is the task overwhelming? Ignore that part. Only focus on the first step. Is the task scary? Ignore that too and stay focused on the first step. Is it not the best timing? Forget it. Timing will never be perfect. Take the first step. The way ahead is hard? Too bad. Take the first step anyway. Last week, I had to write a paper for a school critiquing the use of Cohen's kappa and factor analysis in a research study. I had no idea what this stuff was, let alone how to critique it. The way ahead was daunting. I showed up, went to my desk, took the first step, and read the chapter.

Review: Get Started

Tools	Things to think about
Show up	Where do you need to go to show up?
Take the first step	Think of a big project you want to do. What is the first step?

Keep Trying

Success is the ability to go from one failure to another with no loss of enthusiasm.

—Winston Churchill

"Get back on the horse" is code for keep trying. When one of life's challenges presents itself to you, lick your wounds, get up, brush the dust off, and get back on the horse. Falling off the horse can happen in many ways. If you messed up that important presentation, learn from the experience and then go do another presentation. If you lose a client, figure out whether they were actually a good fit or if you did something to cause them to leave. Then go find another client. If your marketing strategy doesn't work, analyze why and develop a new strategy.

Here is the secret to getting back on the horse: Learn from the fall. Whatever form the fall takes, learn something from falling off. Then try again but incorporate what you learned. How many times do you think

Olympic skating champions fell on their butts before they perfected their quadruple jumps? They jump, they fall, and they learn over and over. They have the ability to get back up and try again and again. If you don't learn from the fall, you'll probably never stay on the horse.

This doesn't mean to keep trying if the endeavor is not worth it or not paying off in the way you had hoped it would. If you learned something from the fall that tells you to move on, then move on. If you learned that you need to approach the endeavor in a different way to achieve your goals, then reevaluate and make a shift.

Effort Alone Is Not Enough

I live in a small town in New Mexico where, a few years ago, we had one good independent local bakery. They eventually went out of business, even though they worked hard. They worked and worked and worked but did the same thing over and over again. Half their baked goods were doughy and dense. The other half were delicious, but they kept making the ones that were doughy and dense even though they got feedback from the community that half their baked goods were inedible. They didn't listen.

They were persevering, but they weren't being tenacious. They weren't pivoting. They weren't looking for new ways to improve their business. They weren't listening to feedback. They just kept doing the same thing over and over again. I approached them several times to make suggestions, but they just blew me off. Finally, the bakery closed.

Effort alone is not enough. If you have a business, you need to figure out what your customer wants. You need to listen to feedback. You need to be able to make changes. If something isn't working, you need to pay attention. If your business seems to be failing, you need to evaluate and understand why.

Two years later, we got a new bakery. They too work hard, but they also pay attention to what the community responds to. Before they opened, I saw an advertisement for their shop on YouTube. They created a beautiful welcoming interior and added a small conference room anyone in the community could use for meetings and workshops. When COVID-19 restrictions temporarily shut them down, they cut a hole in the side of the building and offered drive-through services. Then, when COVID-19 restrictions were lifted slightly, and they were allowed to serve food outside, they made a patio in the parking lot. They faced every hardship that hit and came up with innovative solutions that probably saved their business. It wasn't just their hard work that kept them in business, but their willingness to innovate, to change direction, to listen to, and respond to feedback.

Adapt what is useful, reject what is useless, and add what is specifically your own.

—Bruce Lee

Review: Keep Trying

Tool	Things to think about
Effort alone is not enough	Describe a project at home or work where you keep trying but don't seem to be getting anywhere.
	How could you change your approach to this project?

The Small Bite Approach

To build a successful business, you must start small and dream big.
—Aliko Dangote

A little bit every day goes a long way. It's true. A huge task that overwhelms you is not going to get finished in one go. The traditional approach is to chunk it. Break the task up into smaller tasks. For example, a new small business owner might be looking at how to market the business. The options are endless—social media, a professional website, online advertising platforms, television, and movie theater and telephone advertising. There are sponsorships and community giving. There is no limit to the options for marketing.

Several years ago, I took a workshop on how to leverage social media marketing. The instructor introduced us to many different avenues to market on the Internet. Many of these methods were free or cost-friendly. There were so many ideas that I was overwhelmed, but I knew I needed to develop my social media savvy, so I hung in there. I had no idea where to start. Finally, the instructor said, "Don't try to do it all. Pick one thing that makes sense for you or your business and go from there." I decided to start with a web page. If you are job hunting, you might start with LinkedIn.

The classic approach is to take your big overall goal and break it down into a series of small mini-goals. Finish and celebrate each mini-goal before going on to the next. This works especially well in areas such as strategic planning, business development, career change, gardening, and weight loss.

However, today's world is not always a classic one or one that moves slowly enough to accommodate the small bite approach. It is possible that taking small bites is not the best solution for you or your business, especially for us outliers. Sometimes, we have to jump in and tackle everything at once, which can be exhilarating. Jumping in requires coordination, possibly a team, possibly a focus point, and a specific desired outcome. Jumping in often works well for new situations that feel huge, such as a launching a startup, rolling out a new program, forming a merger, or introducing a new product or location.

Review: The Small Bite Approach

Tool	Things to think about
Small bite approach	Describe a project from your work or personal life that might benefit from using a series of mini-goals.
	Describe a project from your work or personal life where it might be best to just jump in.

Do One More

Many of life's failures are people who did not realize how close they were to success when they gave up.

—Thomas Edison

Give 110 percent. Go the extra mile. Exceed expectations. I hate these expressions. They are trite and superficial, and I'm not sure what they mean. Instead, consider doing just one more.

Push

I was at the gym and pushing the dumbbell over my head for a triceps extension. I was aiming for 10 repetitions. I made it to eight repetitions, and felt I couldn't do any more. My trainer encouraged me to keep going. "Just do one more," he said. I pushed, and it seemed my muscles were about to buckle. "Push," Sean urged. I pushed through, feeling the burn, knowing I was probably using sloppy technique, but I got one more. Every workout after that, I did one more. Today I'm proud to say that I have good arms.

Coach George Allen became famous for turning losing sports teams into winning teams with his philosophy of "do one more." Coach Allen believed the difference between winning and losing was so slight, a second effort, a little extra push, or just one more often determined the outcome of a game.

The movie *Hacksaw Ridge* tells the true story about Army Medic Desmond Doss during a horrific battle in the Second World War. Doss was a conscientious objector who held deep spiritual beliefs and refused to carry a gun. In the movie, Doss stayed behind on the ridge to rescue wounded soldiers. Each time he saved one, he would ask God to allow him to save just one more. Doss ultimately rescued 75 souls.

Doing one more is often not easy. It's about giving a small bit of extra effort. It's a push. It's about pushing just a little more. A bit of extra effort. We might need help to do one more. Sometimes, we need a trainer or a coach or God to urge us on. Just one more, regardless how little can add up to a miracle.

Character consists of what you do on the third and fourth tries.

—James A. Michener

Review: Do One More

Tool	Things to think about
Push	Describe something—a task, situation, project—where you usually stop when it becomes difficult. What would you need to be able to push just a tiny bit harder?

Be in the Moment

Bulldogs have been known to fall on their swords when confronted by my superior tenacity.

—Margaret Halsey

Stop and smell the roses. Be in the moment. Enjoy the ride. These are yet more trite expressions, but I happen to like them, and I think I understand them. Life is short—eat ice cream. We've all heard these various metaphors for living. However, the journey metaphor is often clouded by the tasks of living. I know this is true for me with writing, coaching, gardening, dog-walking, weightlifting, practicing Tai Chi, and trying to manage my weight. My life often becomes a list of things to accomplish.

Enjoy the Ordinary

One beautiful day, not too hot and not too cold, I was walking our little yappy dog, enjoying the view of South Mountain and the high plains. I felt good, muscles moving. I suddenly got the smell of something sweet and delicious. Chocolate flowers that had popped up in an empty field. Perhaps they were rogue seeds from my garden. Chocolate flowers only open in the morning. I stopped to take in the heady fragrance. It was a glorious moment. I lingered a bit more, and in that lingering, the dog walk became more than just an ordinary task. It became something to savor on its own merit. It became a journey to enjoy.

To enjoy the journey or be in the moment means different things to different people. It is difficult for some people to even fathom the concept, let alone actually do it. And, how does this relate to tenacity? I think it allows moments of recovery, maybe recuperation. It can be reenergizing, especially if your work projects have been arduous. By taking the time to notice special moments, we can find a bit of pleasure, a bit of space, a moment to breathe, to relax, to appreciate, to feel grateful—all of which will help us to carry on.

Review: Be in the Moment

Tool	Things to think about
Enjoy the ordinary	What is something ordinary that you do every day? How could you turn this ordinary something into a moment of enjoyment?

Get Community

Every person is defined by the communities she belongs to.

—Orson Scott Card

No man or woman is an island. To me, a community is a group of individuals connected to each other by one or more attributes. Our community should be a reflection of who we want to be. For example, if you want to become a veterinarian, go join some sort of veterinarian group. Every career has a group. If you want to learn how to bungee jump off high bridges, go join a bungee jumping club. Scuba diving is a perfect example. There are diving clubs, associations, and even group dive trips. When it comes to career change, finding community is an important part of the process. When it comes to tenacity, finding community can be a boon.

Surround Yourself

Surround yourself with others who have tenacity. It's inspiring. It makes you want to go do things just by looking at what they're doing. Those who have tenacity and enthusiasm for life can bolster our own inner sense of excitement and enthusiasm and give us the backbone to keep trying. Don't underestimate how powerful the encouragement and support from a community of like-minded people can be. A connection to community can give us the energy to keep going, especially when you're feeling like you just want to give up. It can also be a place we can find a sense of belonging.

I belong to a writer's group that meets monthly. They also offer workshops, ongoing classes, and lectures. Every time I go to a meeting or lecture or workshop, I come home inspired and energized. And, it's not just listening to the program; it's sitting next to other writers of all ages and abilities. There's room for everybody, and I don't feel any competition between members. I find it uplifting and inspiring to be around them. I go as often as I can.

Writers especially can feel isolated and fall into that trap of "What do I have to say? Why is what I have to say important? Why would anyone want to read what I write?" But, being around a group of people who are also excited about literature, about what they're writing, about stories and life, validates me and helps me recognize those qualities in myself. Through my connection with these other writers, I gain a renewed sense of purpose and confidence and joy in the process of writing. After my meetings, I always notice that I am standing a little taller. And, I keep writing.

Other benefits of belonging to groups and communities are that they often provide resources and opportunities for feedback, as well as assistance with whatever kind of obstacle you might be facing.

> *Surround yourself with people that reflect who you want to be and how you want to feel. Energies are contagious.*
>
> **—Rachel Wolchin**

Get Rid of the Vampires (or At Least Minimize Contact)

While positive people give you energy and inspire you, negative people can drain you. They are the *vampires* who suck the joy, enthusiasm, and inspiration out of you. The way to identify a vampire in your life is by observing how you feel when you are around them. If you feel consistently drained, discouraged, insecure, agitated, angry, sad, or disappointed when you are around them, you may want to reconsider that relationship.

Vampires are powerful creatures. They have the power to destroy tenacity in other people. I met a girl once who was training to be a competitive bodybuilder. I saw her again a year later and learned that she had stopped training. She explained that someone had told her she "could only win if all the other girls were fat." She believed she could win, at least on the local level, but that statement haunted her and zapped her enthusiasm.

Vampires also have the power to rewire our brain. If a vampire friend or family member says something negative to us over and over, with time, we may start believing it. Imagine if you heard someone tell you over and over, "You can't do that."

A friend and colleague once told me that her new year's resolution was to get rid of all the vampires in her life. She wanted to break contact with all the people who told her that her dreams weren't possible, and that she should be happy and satisfied with what she had. It may not be possible to completely get rid of the vampires in our life. They may be relatives or coworkers. But if you can, I encourage you to, at the least, minimize contact with them. It is OK to love your vampires, especially if they are family members. Just guard yourself against their power.

Beware of Groupthink

In an old black-and-white film called *The Abilene Paradox*, a family is sitting around the TV in the hot, sweaty, nasty living room. Someone says, "Why don't we drive to Abilene?" And, everyone agrees to go. They all get in the hot, sweaty, nasty old car and drive to Abilene. When they get there, they stop for iced tea, but it's so hot in Abilene that the ice cubes melt, so the tea is tepid and watered down. They finish their tea and drive back home where they get back in front of the TV. Someone says, "Man, that was a nasty trip. Why did we go?"

Well, you know why they went! They went because someone in their group suggested it. Everybody agreed to do something because they thought everyone else wanted to do it, but the truth is that nobody wanted to do it. This is an example of groupthink.

Groupthink is usually defined as a group of people with good intentions who want to have conformity and harmony. The members of the group all agree and make decisions even when the decisions make no sense. Groupthink will kill tenacity in a heartbeat, as well as our creativity. Groupthink will not allow us to keep trying and learning and trying again. That would rock the boat and create disharmony.

Groupthink involves the desire to be part of the group, to belong. We outliers are vulnerable to this. It can cause us to give up our own ideas to fit in. The only tenacity that is allowed will be the tenacity decided upon by the group. Individual tenacity will be seen as stubbornness and a challenge to the group.

If you find yourself in a groupthink situation, get out. If you want to reform a groupthink situation, be prepared for a long run with hard evidence.

Review: Get Community

Tools	Things to think about
Surround yourself	What community do you belong to? If you are not part of a community, describe one that might be interesting or energizing for you.
Get rid of the vampires (or at least minimize contact)	Describe the vampires in your life. How might you begin to remove them from your life?
Beware of groupthink	Describe a time when you acquiesced to the majority to preserve peace and harmony.

Beware: The Universe Will Test You

There will be times when we should give up. Or rather, there will times when we should move on.

Back when I was an undergrad, I was majoring in chemistry, with the intention of going to medical school to become a psychiatrist. Although I was surrounded by people who were willing to help and encourage me, I struggled and struggled. The other students were able to get straight A's even while partying every night. It became clear that working harder was not enough. I finally had to admit to myself that not only was I was not good at chemistry, but I didn't like it.

Admitting I wasn't good at chemistry was devastating. I believed that I had to be a psychiatrist, and that the world expected me to go this route. I had my heart set on this path. As the child of a depressed mother, I had to save all depressed and oppressed housewives. My mother never had this expectation for me, but I felt I would be letting her down if I did not become a psychiatrist. Not following through on that expectation felt like a crushing failure. I had to reconcile that.

All science students had to write papers, which I *was* good at, so I often helped my classmates write their papers. I enjoyed writing and had kept a daily journal since I was 12 years old. The University of Arizona had an excellent journalism and creative writing program, so I changed my major. I liked my writing classes and eventually recognized that my *dream* of becoming a psychiatrist was a false expectation I'd levied upon myself. Instead of continuing to push in that direction, the real challenge was for me to recognize that I needed to let go and move on.

After I graduated and joined the Army, I was faced with an opposite kind of tenacity challenge. Being a Military Police Officer was easy for me, so I never pushed myself. But, I was restless. I tried at one point to get into Public Affairs. Instead of being tenacious after being denied that transfer, I dropped the idea. I had a good position with the Military Police and the future was bright, whereas I would have had to start from the beginning in Public Affairs. I was reluctant to be a beginner again.

As Hamlet should have said, "To be or not to be tenacious—that is the question."

CHAPTER 6

Have Faith

Sometimes all you need is a big leap of faith.

—**Sean Bean**

Have faith. Keep the faith. Faith may now be more necessary in today's world than ever—both at home and in business—as we move toward a global economy, deal with uncertainty, and watch technology changing at breathless rates. Understanding how faith works, the forms it takes, and how we implement it can be a factor in how we succeed. Don't believe me? Oh not O of little faith. Read on.

Have Faith: What Does It Mean?

Faith embraces many truths which seem to contradict each other.

—Blaise Pascal

For me, faith is believing in something you cannot prove. You can't see it, touch it, feel it, or smell it, but it is there. Classic definitions of *faith* often deal with God or religion and define it as complete trust or confidence in someone or something, a strong belief in God or the doctrines of a religion (Oxford Dictionaries). Another definition involves an allegiance to duty or a person, loyalty (Merriam-Webster.com). Faith is also expressed as confidence or trust in a person or thing, faith in another's ability (Dictionary.com). I like this last definition, but all the definitions are good. And, you are invited to develop your own definition.

Do We Need Faith?

The underlying core of faith is hope. It is the expectation of good things to come (wanderlustworker.com). My biological father was an atheist. When he was on his deathbed, he was afraid because "nothing was on the other side." There was no hope for him in death. My mom was a devout Catholic. When she was on her deathbed, she saw the priest and seemed calm because she believed she was going to heaven. She had hope for something better.

Do we need faith beyond religion?

I believe we need to believe and have faith in something. Besides, faith is useful. Faith will help us when we don't know what to do, when we are scared, when the odds are against us. Faith will help us rebound when we fail, feel strong when everyone else is telling us different. Faith will help us find our way when we are confused. Faith will help us stay strong when something feels wrong or when faced with violating what we believe in. Faith will help us face death or even start a business.

Faith can be a calming factor and help us make decisions or solve problems. Faith can help us find a sense of purpose if finding purpose is important to us.

Have Faith When the Chips Are Down

Faith is taking the first step even when you don't see the whole staircase.
—Martin Luther King Jr.

Nothing is certain. Sooner or later, the chips will fall. Bad things will happen. This is when our true character will come out. My mother lived with my abusive, alcoholic biological father for 20 years. He isolated her out in the backwoods of Alaska, with no vehicle or community. She was totally dependent on him and had three daughters to take care of. When she consulted a priest, the priest told her, "This is your cross to bear." The chips were down for my mom. What did she do? She applied to be a foster parent. She told nobody about my biological father, except the priest. Everyone else adored my biological father, for he was a charmer to everyone else. Plus, as abusive as he was, he didn't hurt children. My mom took care of us the best she could and, in addition, took care of abused foster children. She had faith that life would get better.

When my mom and biological father divorced, the IRS knocked on the door and confiscated the house, the property, all the belongings, everything. The IRS drained the bank accounts and garnered my mom's little stipend from the foster agency. It seemed my biological father had not paid income taxes for many years. The IRS left my mom penniless and responsible for back taxes into the thousands of dollars. The chips were down again for my mom. So far down it hurts to write this. What did she do? She got a job and volunteered for a hotline for abused women. Later, we convinced her to go to college. She had faith things would get better. She believed.

When the chips fall for us, what will we do? There is no way to know until the time comes. There are two types of situations when the chips are down. There are the chips-are-down-slow situations and the chips-are-down-fast situations.

Know When to Hold

When the chips are down slow, hold. This is the time to have faith that things will get better. Take a moment to see what happens. It's not the time to make decisions. It may be time to cry or seek solace. These types of situations usually have long-term impact. It is the time to remember what we believe in and stay the course, as pilots say. Hold. Let our values and beliefs come forward and guide us. Examples of chips-are-down-slow situations are the death of a loved one, an unexpected divorce, getting laid off, becoming permanently injured, potentially losing our life savings when the stocks plummet, losing our house, witnessing something horrific, or our business going bankrupt.

Sometimes, we need help for these types of situations, whether it's self-help, a friend's or family member's help, or professional help. Sometimes, we feel a chips-are-down-slow situation reflects who we are. Wrong. The situation does not define us. Hold steady. We need to lean on what we believe in and restore faith in ourselves. Sometimes, we don't know what to do in a chips-are-down-slow situation. It seems there are no answers. It seems there is only uncertainty. That is the time for us to hold. Wait. Hunker down and reflect on options.

Know When to Fold

When the chips are down fast, fold. This is time to take action, when we need to have faith in ourself, our training, or our gut instinct. Chips-are-down-fast situations usually are those that need immediate, sometimes drastic action. These situations can have lasting impact, but usually the intent of our reaction is just to survive. Examples of chips-are-down-fast situations are emergencies, negative performance appraisals, losing a case or an account, financial setbacks but not bankruptcies, a tarnished image or reputation, a change in business conditions, a drop in sales, or a failure to get hired.

In a chips-are-down-fast emergency, taking action often means being prepared and taking swift, immediate action. The key to this is being prepared. Sound familiar? Being prepared and taking immediate action in an emergency is not the reflective, deeper faith required in chips-are-down-slow situations. It requires the faith that comes from knowing what to do. Now.

Other chips-are-down-fast situations allow more time to decide what to do but still need us to take action and move forward. Take a moment to be sad or disappointed and then get moving. Start applying for a new job. Try for the promotion again. Seek another client. Have the faith to continue. Experiment with new ways. Many now-famous authors were rejected multiple times before they ever published a book. Martin Luther King Jr. once said, "If you can't fly, then run, if you can't run then walk, if you can't walk then crawl, but whatever you do, you have to keep moving forward."

Sometimes, a chips-are-down situation means retreating, folding your cards, letting go, getting out of dodge. It's when we know that it's not going to work, that continuing would be fruitless. Perhaps it is our gut instinct that's telling us. Perhaps we have proof. Perhaps we see the writing on the wall that *it* will fail. That is the time for us to have the faith, to suck up our losses and fold. It is the time to have the faith that we can try again. We can succeed next time. We take a little time to recover and move forward. Some people call this process *failing fast*.

I once asked a billionaire entrepreneur at a conference how he recovered from failure. He said he didn't bother recovering. He had faith he would succeed at something but wasn't sure at what. He just moved forward.

When the chips are down, slow or fast, it can help to seek out our support systems. This could be friends, family, colleagues, business partners, or professional groups, and most of all, what we believe in, our faith. It is important to seek out support that is actually helpful. Stay away from negative people who discourage us or those vampire people who suck the energy from us or the naysayer people who doubt us. Also beware the positive people who coddle and soothe us.

When the chips are down, let's remember when to hold and when to fold.

It's easy to have faith in yourself and have discipline when you're a winner, when you're number one. What you got to have is faith and discipline when you're not a winner.

—Vince Lombardi

Review: Have Faith When the Chips Are Down

Tools	Things to think about
Know when to hold	Describe a time when you had to believe that things would get better.
Know when to fold	Describe a time when you had to admit defeat and move on.

Have Faith in Yourself

Painting is a faith, and it imposes the duty to disregard public opinion.

—Vincent Van Gogh

I have met so many clients who simply do not believe in themselves. If we don't have a basic belief in ourselves, we will probably struggle in having faith of any kind.

Know When You've Done a Good Job

My client BJ came to me for career coaching. He felt he was failing at work. He said he wasn't good enough.

"What evidence do you have of this," I asked.

"My boss never tells me I've done a good job," BJ said. This was the real problem. BJ relied on other people to tell him he did a good job. He had no faith in himself. However, when pressed, he could not provide any real evidence that he wasn't good enough. On the contrary, the evidence said the opposite. He received excellent performance appraisals. His work was admired by others. He met deadlines. He supported other teams.

I asked him the key question: "BJ, how do you know you've done a good job?"

"I don't know," BJ said. "People tell me."

To have faith in ourselves, we must know when we've done a good job. Like everything else, this takes practice. Start by thinking about a project, a task, or something you want to do. Before you start, think about the criteria for the project.

BJ started developing criteria for his work. The interesting part is that BJ was already doing this at home. He was a woodworker and had faith in his work and ability. He knew when his pieces turned out well. He didn't need anyone to tell him he'd done a good job. He also knew he could tackle almost any woodworking project handed to him. When it came to woodworking, validation of a job well done came from within him. He started writing down criteria for his office work and, with time, began developing faith in himself. Having criteria is not the faith part. It's the start.

It's always a good feeling when other people praise us. But don't depend on it. There will always be those bosses who don't praise or for whom nothing is good enough. There will always be parents who will say that you can do better. There will always be friends and colleagues whose loud opinions may drown ours. There will always be the in-groups whose style and memes seem better. None of this will bother us when we develop our own criteria for what is good.

Special note for businesses: Tell your people when they've done a good job. Show appreciation. Most people don't leave their jobs; they leave their bosses. The reason is usually because they don't feel appreciated.

Talk to the Negative Voice

I think we all have a negative voice, something inside us that says we aren't good enough or we are stupid or we don't deserve it. Some folks call it the inner critic. Other folks call it a saboteur. Others call it a protective instinct. I call it George. To build faith in ourselves, we must learn to ignore this negative voice. Not all the time, but most.

How to manage a negative voice? First, become aware of it. Listen for it. What is it telling you? Are there specific times when the negative voice seems louder or stronger?

Second, acknowledge it. Our negative voice is not going to disappear. It may fade into the background, but it will always linger there. So, talk to yourself. Say hello to the inner critic. Or in my case, "Hello, George." Listen to what it tells you. If it is criticism, say thank you for that perspective. If it is saying, "You can't do it," say, "Thank you for the warning."

Third, now challenge it. Ask yourself, like I asked my client BJ, for the evidence. OK, inner critic, what proof do you have? Offer the inner critic proof it is wrong. Think of all the good things you've accomplished. "You see, George, you're wrong."

Fourth, send that inner critic–negative voice to a timeout. Tell it to go away for now and sit in a corner. "Just sit quiet, George."

Fifth, take small steps. Develop criteria for a good job. Take a step. Evaluate. Perhaps, revise the criteria. Take another step.

We really can't see or touch our negative voice. To attempt talking or even reasoning with it can feel ludicrous. It works though. I've seen clients use this method. I've used this method myself, thus George. It is an unusual way to build faith in ourselves. Here's the magic: We are actually teaching that negative voice to have faith.

Notice What You Do Well

For some reason, people who do not have faith in themselves often don't remember what they do well. They especially don't remember the small things. BJ had totally forgotten that staff from other departments considered him the go-to person for budget analysis. A small thing perhaps, but when he recalled this, he beamed. BJ started to make notes in his journal, a bound notebook with numbered pages and graph lines like engineers use. He noted his criteria for his projects and reports. He checked them off and highlighted them in yellow when he met the criteria. He decided to also note when other people complimented him, but those notes were highlighted in blue. His goal was to gather more yellow highlighting than blue.

BJ is an analyst and pushed his journal highlighting even further. He started noting what impact his projects had and highlighted that in green for high impact and pink for low impact. He wanted to analyze how meaningfully his time was spent. After a year, he could flip through his journal and describe in detail all the times he had done a good job and what that good job meant for the organization.

It's not necessary to track your work like BJ did. But, consider creating a way to remember what you did well. I do before-and-after pictures of my garden.

Take a Risk

We talk a lot about taking action and moving forward. I read somewhere that faith without action is only wishful thinking. However, sometimes we have to take a risk. When we take a risk, there is a chance something will go wrong. Failure. There may be consequences.

Start small. For example, say no to your boss but say it gently or say, "I don't think so." Call a customer. Ask one question in a meeting. Smile at a stranger.

Take a slightly bigger risk. Volunteer to work on a project nobody else wants. Invest a small amount of money. Apply for that job. Tell your significant other how you feel.

When we take a little risk, we build more confidence and faith in ourselves. It provides proof to that negative voice that yes, we can. If we take a risk and something fails, it's OK. Learn from it, adjust, and keep moving forward. Think about it. Most things in life have an element of risk. Aren't we taking a risk when we fall in love?

Only the person who has faith in himself is able to be faithful to others.

—Erich Fromm

Review: Have Faith in Yourself

Tools	Things to think about
Know when you've done a good job	Think about something you do well. How do you know you've done well?
Talk to the negative voice	What does your inner critic say to you? How do you usually respond to your inner critic?
Notice what you do well	Make a list of 20 things you do well.
Take a risk	What is risky for you?

How: Have Faith in Others

It's not faith in technology. It's faith in people.

—Steve Jobs

Perhaps, I am naïve, but I believe in people. Yes, there are people who will disappoint or hurt me, but I don't believe that's the norm. In the long run, I believe in the basic goodness of people.

Let Others Do It

Long ago, I had a director who was a good boss but had no faith in his people. This especially pertained to reports. Every time we gave him a report, he took his red pen and rewrote it. It was not a matter of accuracy or format. He said he didn't believe anyone could write the reports as well as he could. At first, I worked hard to get the reports perfect. Never happened. He always rewrote them. The joke was that he was changing the report from happy to glad. Then, I quit trying. I didn't even check the spelling.

"Why are you giving me such sloppy reports?" the director asked me.

"Why not? You're going to change everything anyway," I said. "I don't mind if you're my secretary."

Perhaps this director was a perfectionist. Perhaps he was a narcissist. Perhaps he had a boatload of issues, such as trust or insecurity. Who knows? But, the end result is that he did not display faith in his staff. He didn't believe in us. In return, the staff did not give their best to him. They did not believe in him. This form of faith is somewhat of a paradox, like the old maxims you have to give respect to be respected, or you have to give love to be loved. You have to have faith in others for them to have faith in you. Let others write the darn reports.

Do Not Rely on First Impressions

I've been told many times by friends and colleagues that they are good judges of character, and that they usually judge with first impressions. "I can size a person up in a glance," people sometimes say. This means whatever first impression we make will be the impression that will last. First impressions are powerful things and influence many of our decisions: who we date, who is likable, who is hirable, who is trustworthy. First impressions are typically made in less than a second. And, they are often wrong.

Consider practicing the art of tabula rasa, which means *blank slate* in Latin. Let's meet people without forming first impressions. Let's allow people to come to us with a blank slate. Let's learn about the other person, perhaps forming a relationship before forming an opinion. Let's give them time before we form an impression. Give them a chance.

This relates to the biggest lament I hear from millennials. "Nobody is listening to us" or "Everyone thinks we are lazy and act entitled" or "The minute we walk in the door, the other person sizes us up and dismisses us."

On the flip side, I've heard employers say, "I rely on my first impressions and will hire accordingly." So, an older person walks in, and the hiring manager thinks, too old, not technologically savvy—and doesn't hire. Or, the millennial walks in, and the hiring manager thinks, too entitled—and doesn't hire. All bogus reasons for not hiring and based on a first impression of less than a second. Stop. Put first impressions aside.

To adopt a practice of tabula rasa is a unique form of faith. It is faith in humanity, a belief that people are essentially good. It is something we can't see or touch. Again, perhaps this is naïve. Perhaps it goes against the primalness in us designed to protect. But, as our world becomes more and more global, we need this form of faith more and more.

Practice Random Acts of Kindness

One morning, a client met me for a session. She was aglow and beaming.

"The person in front of me in the drive-thru lane paid for my coffee," she said. We talked about this for the entire session. The surprise, the unknown benefactor, and the inability to thank the person. "A perfect stranger paid for my coffee!" It was what folks sometimes refer to as a random act of kindness.

Some people practice random acts of kindness because it's trendy or to impress folks who might be watching. But, anonymously or in secret? Try it. For a moment, the universe changes. My client said it created an urge in her to do something nice.

Of course, it doesn't have to be coffee. It could be any act of kindness. But, to get the full effect, it must be done in secret. Keep it small. These random acts relate to faith in a subtle way. It's another way to restore faith in humanity.

Review: Have Faith in Others

Tools	Things to think about
Let others do it	Describe a time when you accepted the work of someone else when you felt you could have done it better.
Do not rely on first impressions	Describe a time when your first impression of a person was wrong.
Practice the art of tabula rasa	How could you practice tabula rasa?
Practice random acts of kindness	What random act of kindness could you do?

How: Have Faith in Your Vision

Anybody who has been seriously engaged in scientific work of any kind realizes that over the entrance to the gates of the temple of science are written the words: "Ye must have faith."

—Max Planck

Your personal vision is how you commit to living your life. Your business vision is how you commit your resources toward a goal. Do you have a vision?

Visualize Your Vision

Remember that hope is at the core of faith? Well, I define *vision* as hope for the future. My vision is, "This is my life—do not waste it." My vision inspires me to try new things, to have adventures, to love fully and allow myself to be loved. My vision is also a reminder of my own mortality and the fleeting time I have here on Earth. Each time I repeat my vision, it also brings me joy. It gives me faith I am on the right path.

Consider creating your own vision for your life. Try describing it. Keep it to one sentence. For inspiration, look up vision statements of well-known companies. Google's vision is "to organize the world's information and make it universally accessible and useful." Hope for the future, faith in the future.

If you can't describe your vision, take a moment to imagine what you hope for your future. Start with the words, *I will...* I usually ask my clients to do this. Here's what some have said.

- I will fight for social justice.
- I will create new forms of energy.
- I will design the kitchens of the future.
- I will organize lives.
- I will defend the waterways.

Each one of these *I will* statements reflects the hope these clients have for their future. Again, it can't be touched or seen. It's faith in the future. You don't need a fancy analysis or special training to create your own vision. Simply fill in the blank and see what happens: I will _____.

Faith makes you a businessperson of action.

—Zechariah Newman

Review: Have Faith in Your Vision

Tool	Things to think about
Visualize your vision	I will _____. (personal vision) I will _____. (business or career vision) I will _____. (relationships vision) I will _____. (creative vision)

Have Faith in Your Faith

My faith helps me overcome such negative emotions and find my equilibrium.

—Dalai Lama

Your faith is right for you. Your beliefs are right for you. There is one caveat: Your faith and beliefs must not hurt others.

Practice What You Preach

If we truly have faith in who we are, our values, and our belief system, we need to behave like we do. We need to practice what we preach. To walk the talk. When we do this, it reinforces our beliefs and makes us stronger.

Carla is a devout Christian. She lets you know it too. Don't curse around her. Don't ask her to take down the religious pictures that fill her office. Don't ask her to work late if it's church night. Yet, she was the first to blame others when things went wrong, and the first to take the credit when things went right. She had a sign on her office door: Love thy neighbor. That's where she often stood when she gossiped about her coworkers and boss.

Carla came to me for career coaching because she wanted to get promoted. She told me she couldn't get promoted because everyone was against her religious beliefs. We spent months examining what her religious beliefs meant and how it impacted her getting promoted. One day, Carla came to our usual session, quieter than usual.

"I don't have faith in my faith. I'm not practicing what I preach," she said. "How do I do that?"

"I don't know," I said. "Let's explore that."

We spent many more months on this. Carla also worked with a spiritual advisor at her church. She ultimately moved to another organization where she could start fresh.

Practicing what we preach can be tough. It requires a form of faith that Carla said best: "faith in my faith." It could also be the most difficult form of faith to practice. Sometimes we think we are practicing what we preach, but we're not.

Faith is the essential characteristic that all successful entrepreneurs share. I believe you must bring your whole self to the table if you want to thrive in today's world.

—**Marie Forleo**

Review: Have Faith in Your Faith

Tool	Things to think about
Practice what you preach	Describe what you believe in.
	How do you practice it?

Be Ready: The Universe Will Test You

Sometimes life hits you in the head with a brick. Don't lose faith.

—**Steve Jobs**

Anyone can have faith when life is good. When we are winning. When the whole world loves us. When there is no pain. When there is no consequence. When business is booming. It's another story when the universe tests us. The tests could be as minute as flipping an egg onto the floor, to as torturous as losing a loved one. The tests come in many forms, such as temptation or adversity or challenge. We could think of ourselves as on a hero's journey. We are Sinbad the Sailor passing the test of the seven doors in search of the blue rose to save our true love.

There is no doubt: Just when we don't expect it, we will be tested. Life can be dirty and sneaky as hell. In fact, there is a legend that the closer to God we get, the more the devil tempts us. When the universe tests us, we will show what we are made of. What will we do? Do we know who we are and what we stand for? If we don't know, our faith will wobble; we may lose focus or make decisions we will regret. Do we have the courage to take action? If we don't, our faith is just talk or daydream.

The biggest test of all is when the universe tests our belief in ourselves. This is more than a test. This is an opportunity to prove who we are, to get through the door and grab the blue rose.

Know that our faith will be constantly tested. You pass the test when you continue to believe.

—Suzanne Evans

CHAPTER 7

Lead the Way

Leaders aren't born, they are made.

—Vince Lombardi

Leadership is multifaceted. It shows up in most aspects of our lives, not just in our work lives. Parents, teachers, chief executive officers (CEOs), life coaches, team leaders, social media influencers, sports coaches, older siblings, and so on are all positions that require leadership skills. I didn't intend to become any sort of leader, but life circumstances conspired to put me in leadership positions over and over again.

As the first-born child in a family in which there was little parental supervision, I felt it fell to me to take care of myself and my sisters when my father was drunk or absent, and my mother wasn't available. My early lessons in leadership prepared me for various supervisory roles in the military, and after that, in the corporate world. Now I am the leader in my life as a self-employed coach and author. I may not have a platoon to lead, but I have clients to motivate, readers to inspire, and a little dog with anxiety issues to nurture.

Lead the Way: What Does It Mean?

Leadership is service to others.

—Denise Morrison

The definition of *leadership* for me is the ability to influence others. And, that could mean helping, nurturing, guiding, directing, teaching, modeling, commanding, demonstrating, and so on. The definition is simple, but the ways in which leadership can be exercised are as diverse as the positions leaders inhabit.

Lead the Way: Why?

Power should be reserved for weightlifting and boats, and leadership really involves responsibility

—Herb Kelleher

First and foremost, we need leaders to shoulder the responsibility. Leaders are basically responsible for and to the people who follow them. Leadership provides a structure for organization, whether in a business, government, or home. The leader, by whatever name, represents the group, sets the example, and often makes the decisions. Leaders show us the way. They provide vision for the future.

Take Care of Your People

The growth and development of people is the highest calling of leadership.

—Harvey S. Firestone

Mark is an engineer in a leadership position. He oversees a large staff, but feels it is not his responsibility to defend them or make suggestions about how they could be more successful. He often tells the staff that he is not their babysitter. The staff is left on their own to figure things out: what Mark, the boss, wants and what they, the staff, want. There is little direction or guidance from Mark. One of my coaching clients, Joe, worked for Mark. He left his job, even though he loved his work, because Mark was impossible to work for. Joe said that Mark's team had the highest turnover rate in the company, and that as a result, his teams produced less and experienced more infighting.

Leaders who do not take care of their staff, who do not motivate, encourage, guide, and inspire will always experience dissent and lack of enthusiasm among their team members. Ultimately, these leaders will either lose their employees or have to live with their resentment and poor performance. Uninspiring leaders make it hard for even the most creative, talented, and motivated team member to do their best. Good or bad, we are all consciously and unconsciously influenced by those people in leadership positions. If we are led by an inadequate and uncaring *leader*, even the most determined of us will struggle.

Find Out What Is Important to Them

I was once a manager of a leadership program for an organization that was a contractor for the military. When I first took over, there was a bit of resentment on the part of the staff because they wanted someone they were used to. I had come from the outside and was an unknown entity. I invited each member of my new staff to lunch to get to know them better. At these lunches, I asked each person what was important to them. I got answers like, "I need to be able to run five miles every day before I come to work" and "I want to go to business school." Many expressed their desire to spend more time with their children, and one said that he wanted to make a difference in the world. I was moved by my new staff's candor and wanted to make sure I could accommodate them in a way that aligned with the needs of the organization.

For example, I allowed the employee who wanted to run in the morning to come in an hour later if he made up the hour during lunch or at the end of the day. Ultimately, this staff produced great results, especially the young administrative assistant who wanted to go to business school. The organization's tuition remission program paid for her school, with the stipulation that she align her homework and projects to something we were doing in the office. And, she did it.

Everybody had their little perk, and they were happy. They defended our department. It all worked. They were an outstanding team, the best civilian staff I ever worked with.

Develop Them

As leaders, it is our job to develop the skills, talents, and interests of our people. There is no better sign of a good leader than highly functioning people. The first thing to do is to find out what skills they have and what skills they need or want. Address those needs.

For professional development within an organization, create a plan for each person that addresses their career goals as well as the goals of the organization. What type of professional development? The sky's the limit. The budget may be a limit, but many things don't cost much or are free. There are schools, courses, and all manner of workshops and classes. Use the regular weekly or monthly meetings as a chance to learn. Delegate projects to allow junior leaders to take point and lead a project. Use coaches. Try temporary assignments. Consider degree programs, apprenticeships, mentors, and robust onboarding orientation programs. I encourage you to be creative. One of my clients encourages his staff to do volunteer work to get leadership experience.

The skilled trades usually have formal professional development in the form of apprenticeships. I just had two plumbers out to set up an outdoor spigot for irrigation in my vegetable garden. One plumber said he was the real plumber, and the second plumber said he was the apprentice. Many professions require continuing education, such as the medical, legal, and accounting fields. Usually, it is the individual's responsibility to obtain this professional training, but the leaders need to ensure there is time and resources allowed for this to happen.

For small businesses, the budget is usually a big factor, and professional development sometimes doesn't happen because of this. Or, there is an attitude that the business is too small for professional development. My friend, a chef, takes time to train the staff on new menu items and wine selection right before opening time. Informal apprentice programs, mentoring, and staff meetings could all be considered professional development opportunities.

For those of you with a one-person business, the solopreneurs, keep developing yourself and learning about your business. There are plenty of inexpensive or free resources. They can range from professional organizations to online presentations and how-to videos to audiobooks to local conferences.

The idea is to help people to grow and develop their capacity. Sometimes, a person will not be interested. Maybe they are just out of school and just want to work. Maybe they are about to retire and just want to retire. Maybe their plate is too full at home and it's not the right time. That's all OK. We don't need to push professional development on anyone who doesn't want it or isn't ready.

The signs of outstanding leadership appear primarily among the followers. Are the followers reaching their potential? Are they learning? Serving? Do they achieve the required results? Do they change with grace?

—Max De Pree

Review: Take Care of Your People

Tools	Things to think about
Find out what's important to them	If you are in a leadership position, describe what is important to each person you lead. If you are a parent, describe what your children feel is important. If you are married, describe what your spouse feels is important. If you are a company or family of one, describe what is important to you.
Develop them	How are you supporting or nurturing what's important to the people above?

Adjust Your Leadership Style

I suppose leadership at one time meant muscles: but today it means getting along with people.

—Mohandas K. Gandhi

I have a theory that post-Second World War, corporate American leadership was influenced by all the colonels, generals, and commanders who came back with an authoritative leadership style and brought it into the workplace. It was successful for a while. But, as the world changed, leadership styles had to change also. We still need leaders who know how to take charge, but we also need leaders who can be transformational, more like coaches, teachers, or mentors. We need kinder, gentler leaders, perhaps introvert leaders or what Jim Collins, author of *Good to Great*, refers to as the Level 5 leader.

There is no one perfect leadership style that works for all situations. Leaders need to be able to adjust their style to reflect the times we are living in and to accommodate the new generations entering the workforce. In addition, what makes people happy changes as they age. As effective leaders, we can't put one leadership or one happiness strategy in place and assume it will work for everyone all the time. We must change with the times as well as with the people we're leading.

Check the Situation

Situational leadership, a theory developed by Paul Hersey and Ken Blanchard, describes four types of leadership scenarios. There is the employee who is an expert in their field. You don't have to give them a lot of supervision. Then there's the employee who is highly motivated but doesn't have any experience. They will need more supervision. On the opposite side of the coin, you have the people who are not motivated but have the skills you're looking for, and the people who are neither motivated nor skilled. Each of these situations requires a different type of leadership. Good leaders find out what their team needs and what the situation requires and adjust to it.

Lead From Behind

A leader is best when people barely know he exists; when his work is done, his aim fulfilled, they will say: we did it ourselves.

—Lao Tzu

It is my job as a coach to help my clients achieve success. In my school of coaching, we coach by leading from behind. We allow clients to take the spotlight. We try not to tell clients what to do or what decisions they should make. We help clients lead themselves toward success. This is one way to lead. It's not the only way to lead, but by standing on the sidelines, we may be able to better empower our clients, employees, or team.

It's about getting out of the way, stepping back in victory and stepping up in crisis.

It is better to lead from behind and to put others in front, especially when you celebrate victory when nice things occur. You take the front line when there is danger.

—Nelson Mandela

Review: Adjust Your Leadership Style

Tools	Things to think about
Check the situation	Describe two situations you've experienced, either as a leader or team member, that required two types of leadership.
Lead from behind	Describe a situation where you might lead more effectively if you let others lead the way.

Set the Example

Be a yardstick of quality. Some people aren't used to an environment where excellence is expected.

—Steve Jobs

The most impactful way we can lead is to set the example. Leadership is never about "do what I say, not what I do." When we set the example as leaders, people will emulate what we do. As followers, we will emulate our leaders, perhaps without even realizing it.

Model Excellence

When I was in the military, I always ensured that my uniform was impeccable. It was heavily starched and sharply creased. The saying was that when you first put on your uniform, it was "breaking starch." (I don't think they do that anymore.) I had five pairs of boots that I took to a boot-shining service. I held myself to the highest uniform standard possible so that I could model it for my troops.

Granted, a uniform is a little thing, and possibly a superficial gesture. But, done right and backed up with leadership behavior, it reflects excellence. Of course, the military is not the only place that features uniforms. The theory and use of uniforms could be an entire book by itself. Here, we only want to use it as an example of how to outwardly express excellence.

Model excellence in all that you do. "If you are going to do something, do it well." If that means cleaning a toilet, do it excellently. If that means leading an army, do it excellently. Seek excellence, not power or glory. Model excellence as a leader, and it will be reflected back in your staff, your students, your children, and your club members.

Don't Be a Workaholic

Overwork is this century's cocaine, says Bryan Robinson, PhD, author of *Chained to the Desk*, a guidebook for workaholics. I work with many clients who seem overworked and are required to put in 60 hours a week or more at their job. Most of these clients are baby boomers and older millennials. When they come to me, they are usually seeking a change in their job or career that will give them a better balance between their personal and professional lives. They typically do not want to be working so much. Occasionally, one of these clients turns out to be a workaholic.

A workaholic works all the time. It is a compulsion and makes for bad leadership. It can also impact health and relationships, professional and personal. Being a workaholic doesn't mean good work is being done. Workaholics are famous for doing busywork or redoing someone else's work.

Phoebe was 45 years old when I met her. She was divorced and had two children, whom her ex-husband had full custody of. She got to work at 5 a.m. when the regular start time was 8 a.m. She had lunch at her desk. She worked late every night, often having supper at her desk. She managed a department and was looking to be director, so she doubled her efforts, taking work home every night, getting little or no sleep, and working every weekend. She proudly told everyone that she was a workaholic.

Phoebe rewrote every report that came across her desk. Sound familiar? If there was a lull in the action, she rewrote the reports again. She took lead on every project and conducted every presentation. She became angry and sometimes bullying if questioned by staff, and depressed if questioned by her own boss. By the time I met Phoebe, she was sleeping on the couch in her office instead of going home. Phoebe slapped a folder down in front of me. It was the results of a 360-degree evaluation that included anonymous feedback from her staff and peers.

The feedback was brutal, and at times, downright mean. It basically described Phoebe as a heartless dictator. She had no compassion, no empathy, no concern for others. One comment stated Phoebe's only concern was work, work, work, even if the work made no sense. Another comment said Phoebe only wanted to control everything and everybody. I asked Phoebe how she felt about the feedback.

"They're all wrong!" Phoebe yelled. "We have to work this hard to achieve success! This is a waste of time. I need to get back to work." I referred Phoebe to a therapist.

Yes, Phoebe was an extreme case, and it must have been hell to work for her. That is the impact a workaholic can have on the workplace. They create hell. Workaholics burn out their people and themselves. They do not inspire, they demoralize. They do not set achievable goals, they set unrealistic expectations. They do not empower others, they seek to control. Yes, sometimes we have to burn the midnight oil and put in some extra hours, but that is not the norm.

There are times when a certain amount of overwork is OK. When it is part of our passion. When we are launching a business, developing a new product, creating a piece of art, or engaged in lifesaving rescue work. However, generally speaking, if you work all the time, if you brag that you are a workaholic, find a counselor.

Don't Be a Perfectionist

I also hear people brag that they are a perfectionist. Perfectionism is usually not worth the effort it requires. Very few things need to be perfect. Rocket science, nuclear weapons, legal documents, and situations where lives are at stake probably need to be as perfect as a human can get them. For the rest of life, consider that 80 percent might be good enough. Sometimes I'll work on a project and find I am spending an inordinate amount of time on getting the last details perfect. My husband will often ask me, "Have you reached 80 percent?" And, almost always I have reached above 90 percent. I sigh and stop.

Most of the time, seeking perfection is an exercise in frustration. I think Americans are obsessed with perfectionism: the perfect Thanksgiving, the perfect wedding, the perfect gift, the perfect vacation, the perfect carrot at the farmers market.

From a leadership standpoint, perfectionism deflates creativity and crushes spirits. From a psychological standpoint, perfectionism is often considered just another way to exercise control. As leaders, if we can let go of that level of control, we create the space for our team, group, employees, children, and clients to take risks and grow. We need to make the space for our people to do something on their own. There is always a possibility that by loosening our perfectionist grip, our teams will be able to come up with something better than we could have ever imagined.

Be Accountable

To be accountable means to take responsibility for our own actions, to do what we say we're going to do. In leadership roles, accountability is the acknowledgment and assumption of responsibility for actions, products, decisions, and policies. Be accountable and hold others accountable as well. Establish expectations.

Sometimes a leader is held accountable when someone else is *to blame*. When I was stationed in Germany, one of my young sergeants got into a bad fight in a local bar. My higher-ups were threatening to kick him out of the Army. My job as his platoon leader was to stand with him and support him during a military hearing. I took full responsibility for his actions and said, "He's not the one to blame. I'm the one." They forgave me and him and gave him another chance. I am sure my willingness to stand up for him, to take responsibility, helped in this. He was demoted, but after two years of hard work, he regained his sergeant stripes.

Other areas of accountability include meeting deadlines and keeping promises. In regular circumstances, we have to be accountable for the projects or tasks we take on and for the promises we make. However, the universe is not a perfect place and life happens. If we can't keep a promise or meet a deadline, we need to make it known and assist with developing a Plan B. If it is an emergency or a life-threatening situation, then we need to let it be known and let others develop a Plan B.

Review: Set the Example

Tools	Things to think about
Model excellence	How do you model excellence?
Don't be a workaholic	Describe a time when you were a workaholic or worked for or around a workaholic.
Don't be a perfectionist	In what situations, do you expect perfection?
Be accountable	Describe how you handled a situation when you could not meet a deadline or keep a promise.

Create Teams

The world needs new leadership, but the new leadership is about working together.

—**Jack Ma**

More organizations are working with teams. And, the ones that aren't, should be. As the baby boomers retire and diverse numbers of young people enter the workforce, teams or groups are becoming more and more valuable. Teams bring energy; they are a great source of power and creativity. And from a practical perspective, if one team member leaves, there is still some organizational tribal knowledge left over that can support a new person who is brought in.

I had a client who was a bigwig in the U.S. Forest Service human resources department. She had a huge project she was struggling with and a large staff at her disposal. I suggested that she create a team to work on this project. I didn't tell her how to do it. I just said, "Get a group together in one room and start there." She said that from day one, just bringing everyone around the table together made things go better. She had people representing different disciplines who were helping her and making suggestions.

Person A would make a suggestion, and then person B would say, "Well, that will impact me in this way…and I may have to make adjustments." Adjustments were made, compromises were made, and the project was finally successfully completed.

Create a Balanced Workload

Teams made up of old and young people, and people from different cultures, ethnic backgrounds, sexual and gender orientations, and socioeconomic classes, are generally more original, creative, and innovative. And, teams in which the workload is balanced allow for greater individuality and success. When one or two people are doing all the work, the benefits of a team are usually lost. I hear sometimes from my clients that a team member is not contributing as much.

I remember a time when I was in graduate school and required to work with a team of four other students. Our grade depended on the combined contribution of the team. One team member, Ed, refused to do the same amount of work as the rest of us. The professor told us to work it out. We tried to work it out, but nothing changed. We all received a lesser grade because Ed's lack of contribution pulled us down, which the professor frankly pointed out. The situation starts with the leader—in this case, the professor. Care must be taken that all team members contribute equally.

Yes, there are times when the team is only as strong as the weakest link. Perhaps we should have helped Ed or conducted an intervention or bribed him with pizza. Perhaps we should have explored his strengths. Perhaps we should have considered any mitigating circumstances on Ed's side. But, we were just stupid graduate students who wanted to get an A in the course and didn't do any of those things. The situation should have been structured by the leader, our professor.

Sometimes the work doesn't happen concurrently, and there may be a perception that not everyone is putting in their fair share of the work. For example, person A needs to finish a piece before person B can do their part. When the project first starts, it needs to be made clear that team members could be actively working on the project at different times. It could also mean that specific projects require different amounts of work from different people. This also needs to be made clear.

A balanced workload also means teams need to allow team members to work alone. Not everyone is at their best working with a team. Some people will need to go off and work alone before bringing their ideas and parts of the project to the team.

Establish High-Performance Teams

High-performance teams consistently achieve superior results (think pit crew at a NASCAR race) and typically outperform other teams. High-performing teams are focused on the mission, and usually, each team member has a specific skill set. The mission may represent a set of common values. These teams are accountable, never miss a deadline, and often are innovative. They sometimes take risks and always *have each other's backs*. High-performing teams are often based in servant leadership where the team leaders inspire and serve.

How to create a high-performance team? Forget the forming, storming, norming, performing stages of team-development theory. This theory accounts for how a classic team develops. It is a process of getting a group together who may not get along, establishing the rules or norms of the team, and then performing well as a team. This will get you a good team, but the team needs time to get there, and the results may not always be exceptional. A true high-performing team will perform from day one and consistently achieve an exceptional outcome. Create a high-performing team this way:

- Have a purpose. Put the team on a mission. Make it important. Tell the team.
- "Get the right people on the bus and in the right seats," says Jim Collins, author of *Good to Great*. This means determining what skill sets you need and finding people with those skill sets. Try to keep the number of people to about ten.
- Learn how each team member communicates. Consider a workshop to explore the different communication styles present in the team.
- Learn with each project. Conduct a lessons-learned session after each project. Discuss what went well and what could be improved. What the team could do less of and what they could do more of.

Leadership and learning are indispensable to each other.

—John F. Kennedy

Review: Create Teams

Tools	Things to think about
Create a balanced workload	Describe a time when you were on a team and it seemed like all the work was being done by you and one or two other people.
Establish high-performance teams	Describe the best experience you ever had when working with a team.

Be Ready: The Universe Will Test You

The measure of a man is what he does with power.

—Plato

"We need to ace this inspection," my commanding officer told me. I had just been promoted to first lieutenant and was taking lead on a critical inspection of our company. It was a high-stakes inspection and meant a lot to our newly formed Military Police company. I was proud to get the assignment and eager to prove my worth.

"Yes, sir," I said. "I'll do my best."

"I don't think you're hearing me," he said. "We need to ace this thing." Of course, I heard him. I also heard the menacing undertone in his voice.

"I'll do my very best," I said.

"You need to do better than that," he said. "If we don't ace this, it will reflect on your evaluation report. You'll never make captain."

"Like I said, I'll do my best," I said. "But because I want to, because I want to ace it too, not because you threatened me."

We aced the inspection, and the company commander never threatened me again. He was a bully, responsible for more than 220 military police. He'd confused responsibility with power and intimidation. My mother used to say a person's true character comes out when you give them power or get them drunk. One night at the officers club, the commander got drunk. He was happy and ridiculous at first, like the rest of us. As the night worn on, he became threatening and sullen. I wasn't surprised. We got him home before any fights broke out.

There will come a day when we will be given some measure of power over others. People will come to know us according to how we use that power. The question is, how do we want to be known?

CHAPTER 8

Challenge the System

It is the first responsibility of every citizen to question authority.
—**Benjamin Franklin, according to legend**

Thankfully, the human traits of curiosity and problem-solving, perhaps inborn, have inspired some people to find new and different ways of doing things. In going against the *old ways*, these mavericks (you could also call them outliers) have enabled tremendous human advancement over a span of only 10,000 years—an evolutionarily tiny span of time. But, there are always authority figures around to defend the old ways, often with the use of violence, coercion, and repression. It takes bravery and sacrifice to work toward new ways.

Outliers challenge authority because they often feel they have not been welcomed into the mainstream. And so, they are in the unique position of being able to see when a system is exclusionary or prejudiced or working against people who should be supported. In my case, my experience growing up in Alaska taught me to challenge systems when they weren't working.

I realize my childhood is unusual, and that not everyone would have evolved out of it in the same way I did. However, we all have something to offer that is unique and unexpected, or outside the box. Our individuality, our unique experiences, and mindsets, can show us how to challenge authority when authority is exploitative or outmoded.

To change and grow, to evolve our beliefs and values, not only do we need to challenge outmoded or entrenched systems (beliefs, institutions, governments, and so on.), but we must challenge our own inner oppressive voices and limiting ideologies, beliefs, and values. We must ask ourselves where our beliefs and values came from and whether we still believe (or ever believed) in them. Often our values come straight from our parents and teachers, and we operate unconsciously in accordance with them. Sometimes, we realize we actually don't agree with them. It is up to us to do the inner work (through counseling, meditation, coaching, education, and so on.) that will allow us to break free of our unconscious limiting beliefs. When we do this, we are better able to act and access the courage to challenge authority and change the system when necessary.

Outliers can feel alienated, ostracized, disconnected, and disenfranchised, but it is these feelings that can give the outlier their superpowers. As outliers, we have a perspective that is naturally different. Though we may threaten people and institutions who are determined to uphold the status quo, there are many—employers, colleagues, organizations—who will be attracted to our innovative point of view. We can bring about new ideas and inspire others. By challenging the system, we can challenge what is possible. Without outliers standing up to the notions of what is possible, we would not have the technology we rely on today. We would not fly in airplanes; we would not have satellites or electricity or refrigerators or computers or… You get the point.

Challenge the System: What Does It Mean?

Any intelligent fool can make things bigger and more complex.... It takes a touch of genius—and a lot of courage—to move in the opposite direction.

—Albert Einstein or possibly E.F. Schumacher

Challenging the system means to question assumptions and reject the status quo. It is about looking at things differently and making the world a better place. It is about asking questions and finding answers in new places. Challenging the system is not simply about refusing to follow policy, procedures, or the manager's directives. To do this without purpose or good cause is childish and even potentially harmful. Challenging the system does not involve passive–aggressive behaviors like talking behind someone's back or making visible or audible signs of disdain, such as eye-rolling and sighing, or failing to complete work by the required deadline. This behavior is just rude. Challenging the system is also not about disrespecting or hurting others. It's not about sabotaging work products or other coworkers, or theft of property. Challenging the system is about making things better.

Challenge the System: Why?

By challenging the system, we can help create a new world. Challenge can stimulate growth and curiosity and prompt discovery about the reasons behind things. Without challenge to the status quo, businesses stagnate and often die. This is because businesses need to grow and change as the world changes. Challenging an outmoded system has the power to bring about new ideas and reenergize people. Each generation brings forth something special and adds their spice to the world.

Challenging the system is also about righting a wrong, especially if it involves authority. Authority is human and thus fallible. Sometimes authority figures exploit their position by representing their own opinions and interests. Or, it is a system that is unfair or flat-out wrong. If we are silent, we are potentially consenting. Sometimes we need to speak up.

There is an old adage: What we permit, we promote. A leader alone cannot create vast change. The power of a movement lies in its followers. If we witness someone else being affected or taken advantage of, it may be time for us to stand up and object. Being a silent bystander only permits whatever is happening to continue.

However, it is important to understand the risks involved in challenging authority. Even though I am an advocate for change, I don't necessarily recommend challenging the system to everybody. A single parent with two kids, who might risk losing their job if they challenge the boss, might need a safer way to challenge the system. As a coach, I'm not supposed to tell people what to do. My suggestion to clients who have a lot to lose by challenging their present circumstances is to hunker down, get out of harm's way, and secretly look for another job. There are circumstances in which protesting or objecting is just too dangerous. When the climate is too volatile and the stakes are too high, please protect yourself and your family first.

Leave no authority existing not responsible to the people.
—**Thomas Jefferson**

Learn to Argue

I believe that there's a way to question authority with manners, with dignity. There's no reason to be rude about it
—**Nicolas Cage**

Challenges to the system are not necessarily dramatic protests or hostile interactions. Most challenges are probably born in the hunt for new ideas. If we want to challenge the system, a good place to start is to learn to argue our points. I am not talking about arguing as in arguing with our siblings or spouses when tempers and emotions heat up. I'm talking about the art of argumentation: the action or process of reasoning systematically in support of an idea, action, or theory (Oxford Dictionaries).

If you want to present something to the CEO or your manager, or if you want to buck the system, start gently by making a case for what you're suggesting or proposing by forming reasons, drawing conclusions, and applying them to an argument.

Learn to Debate

The most formal structure for making an argument is in the form of debate. A debate is basically a formal discussion that usually involves two opposing viewpoints. Let's consider Ruby's situation. Ruby is the human resources director in a large organization, and she wants to change a procedure. It's a procedure the previous director tried without luck to change. Ruby wants to try a new approach.

The first thing Ruby does is her homework. She will need to ask questions about the organization. What does it look like? The organization is comprised mostly of engineers, technicians, and analysts. Management is mostly comprised of older engineers. The organization does not like risk. In fact, most of the engineers say it is their job to mitigate risk. Paradoxically, this group also doesn't like change, yet they aspire to be innovative. If ever there was a place or group of people for Ruby to present a well-thought-out case for changing procedures, this is it. This group likely would not respond well to an impassioned plea for change, which is probably what the previous human resources director did.

The second point Ruby needs to consider is how will her new procedure benefit the organization. How much will it cost? What level of effort will it take? Is there any negative impact? It can't be just Ruby's opinion. There must be facts or some sort of supporting evidence. What questions might her engineers ask? What objections might they pose?

Next, Ruby needs to find the right time and place to share her idea for the new procedure. Perhaps it's during a meeting. She needs to stay focused. She must clearly and succinctly introduce her idea and then explain it in terms everyone can understand. This might include providing definitions so that everyone is speaking the same language. (I got in trouble once by using the word *element*. It turned out that my audience and I defined *element* differently.) She might want to discuss her idea point by point. Perhaps include examples. Her argument for the new procedure also needs to be fair. She can certainly emphasize the benefits, but she needs to include the cons as well as the pros.

The time soon comes for Ruby to answer questions and field objections. She not only needs to listen to them, she needs to seek to understand them. It also wouldn't hurt if she were to acknowledge good ideas from others. She needs to be nonthreatening and make it safe for people to object. Then she can provide more evidence for her idea, and gently challenge the other side. Sometimes, at this point, a compromise can be had.

Things to watch out for include our demeanor and use of language. Watch out for emotionalism, such as anger or insults. Passion is allowed. Excitement is allowed. Otherwise, poise under pressure. Also, watch out for rhetorical or leading questions or circular logic. We don't want to try to manipulate our audience with such devices. Be careful about repetition, unless repeating yourself is part of a strategy.

There are many ways to conclude, but it should be nice. Ruby could request a decision, a call to action, or make a simple affirmation such as, "I believe this new procedure is the best thing for us."

The art of debate has helped me change many rules and procedures. I think there are still debate clubs in the schools, but debate is an often-overlooked skill. Debate is more useful than we might imagine. It is especially useful for outliers because we tend to be a little pushy about what we think. Once we learn the art of debate, we can communicate what we think more effectively. We will also be better able to spot vulnerabilities in other people's arguments, such as when salespeople try to convince you to buy something or politicians try to convince you to vote for something. Debate skills can also inspire innovation. Imagine a new idea or product being introduced to a team. A debate could probe its advantages and disadvantages and potentially look at it from a new perspective.

Ruby came to me for career coaching to reinvent her image as a leader. She said she wanted to be able "to represent human resources in engineer language." She especially wanted to be able to present new ideas and be considered an innovative leader. She decided to learn how to debate.

What happened? After about a year, Ruby's procedure was approved along with several other procedures and products she recommended. Ruby is now included on task forces and concept teams whenever there is human impact to consider. Her next career goal is to look at the organization and evaluate its *globalness* in terms of people. Is there diversity? Is there equity?

Practice Critical Thinking

Critical thinking is another part of the art of the argument. Critical thinking is sometimes confused with debate and creative thinking. Debate is about presenting an idea or concept and defending it. Creative thinking is about making something new, whereas critical thinking is about questioning the status quo. It is about analyzing all parts of a product, process, or system to discover how they function separately and together.

In critical thinking, we might apply standards. For example, does the new medicine meet all the required standards? We apply logical reasoning. Does it make sense? We may try to predict what might happen. Critical thinking is about asking questions and challenging our assumptions. Critical thinking is key to innovation.

To get started, identify the basic assumptions. Begin asking questions about those assumptions. For example, many people believe in the basic assumption that breakfast is the most important meal of the day. Many experts support this. Because of this basic assumption, many people eat a large breakfast every day. However, if we challenge this assumption, perhaps it's not entirely true or not true at all. I fall asleep if I eat a large breakfast. Not long ago, I listened to a panel of food experts. The first speaker, a nutritionist, said that breakfast is not the most important meal of the day. She said all meals were important, and that it's important what we eat, not when we eat. She also said that just because a meal was important was not a rationale for overeating. The second speaker, a sports and wellness expert, said it was important to fast for 14 to 16 hours after the last meal of the day, and that the last meal should be eaten according to a person's circadian rhythm or their work schedule. Another nutritionist said the concept of breakfast as the most important meal was only applicable to school children, not adults. Then, a social justice advocate said that any meal was important to a starving person.

Each of the speakers on the food panel challenged the basic assumption of breakfast as the most important meal. Each had their own theory and probably had evidence to support it. Which one is correct? Perhaps all are correct, depending on our situation and nutritional goals. Each speaker brought their own perspective and looked at breakfast under a different microscope. Perhaps you have your own theory.

The idea is to ask questions, be critical of the basic assumption, and develop new ideas. In critical thinking, the core questions to ask include:

- What do we already know about this?
- Why do we do it this way?
- What are the different parts, and how do the parts work together?
- What is the logic behind this?
- What are the credentials of the persons presenting the idea? What field do they represent?
- Could hidden agendas be involved?
- How can we look at this differently?
- Could we reverse this or look at it upside down?
- What if the basic assumption is wrong?
- What is the evidence?
- What biases might be involved?
- How would people in other cultures and socioeconomic groups respond to this?
- What problem does this solve?
- Are there any patterns?
- How does this compare to something else?
- What are the pros and cons?
- How could this be used?
- How can this save the world?

Practice the Art of Appreciative Inquiry

Appreciative inquiry is a different approach to asking questions. It involves the philosophy that a problem is not a problem; it is a mystery to be solved. Appreciative inquiry was developed at Case Western Reserve

University by David Cooperrider and Suresh Srivastva as an approach to how we talk to each other. The main theme of appreciative inquiry is to focus on what is working well. Cooperrider and Srivastva's appreciative inquiry model works like this:

- Discover: Identify processes that work well.
- Dream: Consider what would work well in the future.
- Design: Plan and prioritize what would work well.
- Destiny (or deploy): Carry out the proposed design.

For example, if we wanted to return to the food panel experts, we could request that the experts start with *Discover* and identify what was working well relating to food. Perhaps they all agree that when children are well nourished, they learn better and do better at school. Then, the experts could *Dream* and explore what the world in the future might look like if all children were well nourished. They could ask what might work well pertaining to getting all children the food they need. Next comes *Design*, when our food experts make a plan, determine what's most important, and identify what to do first. Finally, there is *Destiny*, when the plan is carried out.

Nowhere in this plan to get food to the children of the world is there talk of the obstacles and hardships along the way. Once it is time to carry out the plan, those obstacles and challenges will become mysteries to be solved, one at a time. And, it may take a long, long time. But, the inspiration of the Dream, to have well-nourished children in the world, keeps us energized and moving.

Too many times, we focus so much on the problem we become paralyzed and can't move forward. Consider focusing on a dream instead.

Review: Learn to Argue

Tools	Things to think about
Learn to debate	Describe a time when you tried to convince someone else, such as your boss, spouse, or team, to accept your idea.
Practice critical thinking	Using critical thinking, analyze the process for how Americans typically buy groceries.
Practice the art of appreciative inquiry	What is your dream?

Anyone who conducts an argument by appealing to authority is not using his intelligence: he is just using his memory.

—Leonardo da Vinci

Stay Informed

We cannot truly be innovative and challenge the system without knowing what is going on in the world. We must be informed. This will give us the insight as to what the world needs and how the world is changing. In turn, this can give us inspiration and ideas on what to challenge. There are many ways to stay informed. Here are a few to consider:

Observe

Consider people-watching. Think how interesting it is to sit in a public place and enjoy watching the people walk by. We can see fashion trends, relationship behaviors, unconscious habits people have, technology trends, what they might be sipping or munching on, how people walk, what they carry, and how they posture around each other. Perhaps we can overhear snippets of dialogue or get a whiff of someone's cologne. After a time, we are informed about the culture of this place. We can then begin to ask, "What do these people need?"

Consider listening to the news in a more intentional way. Determine how you will receive the news and why. Some people just want to know what is happening and prefer just one news show or one newspaper or one social media platform. Other people want to check out several sources of news and get a sampling of information from each. Some people want to know what other people think about certain topics or issues. Interviews, talk shows, podcasts, and feature columns and editorials in newspapers work well for this.

Consider seeking specialized information about one topic. For example, my friend Cole is a pilot. He likes to be informed about everything aviation. On his computer, he has a news aggregator that pulls stories about aviation. He subscribes to several aviation magazines. He belongs to an aviation association and attends aviation-related events. Every year he flies to Oshkosh, Wisconsin, to attend a huge aviation convention.

Consider becoming informed about ideas and opinions you don't agree with. Check out what the other political party is saying. Find out why investors are predicting peaches will do well when you think peaches will flop. Seek whatever seems strange and try to understand it. This doesn't mean we have to agree. The exercise is to observe, gather information, and become informed.

Participate

When watching or reading the news, form your own opinion. Your opinion is as good as anyone else's opinion. Note where the news came from, fact-check the information, question the news show's or paper's credibility, and note how you emotionally respond to the news. Let the emotion subside and then form your own ideas.

Talk to people. Contact people who have ideas that interest you. Attend talks or lectures and ask questions. Perhaps there are specialty clubs or groups that might help you stay informed about your area of interest. My client Patty is an accountant and interested in investment trends. She participates in a professional investment group to learn about investments from a big-picture perspective. To get a feel for how investments impact what she calls "smart ordinary people," she also participates in an investment club made up of smart ordinary people interested in investing. Patty has made several unusual and successful investment choices based on her interaction with this investment club.

Reach out digitally. Engage in one online media that focuses on news or current events, such as a discussion group or a specialized book club.

Get Global

Learn about the issues in other countries. For example, what are the race issues in other countries? How do their issues differ from the race issues in the United States? How is racism defined in other countries? Which countries are the most racist, the least racist? What are other countries doing or not doing?

Explore foreign industry in America. What large corporations in America are owned by foreign entities? What countries does America have factories in? Is there interaction between the two? What is the impact? What are the possible consequences, both good and bad?

I once listened to a radio show about the making of a t-shirt. From start to finish, the t-shirt went around the world, one place for the cotton, another place for the cotton to be processed into cloth, another place for the cloth to be dyed, another place for the dyed fabric to be cut and sewn into a t-shirt, and another place for screen printing. All these *places* were in different parts of the world! And, then to get to the consumers, the t-shirts first went to a warehouse where they were packaged and shipped around the world to other warehouses before finally being transported to various retail locations.

Review: Stay Informed

Tools	Things to think about
Observe	Where could you go to people watch? How do you stay informed?
Participate	What is your process for forming your own opinions and ideas?
Get global	Think about the things in your life you might have. Where were they made or grown? • Telephone/smartphone • Computer • Car • Clothes you wear • Last movie you watched • Toothpaste • Strawberries or grapes • Plastic bowl • Screwdriver or hammer • Necklace • Camera

Innovate: Think "What If"

To be a philosopher, just reverse everything you have ever been told... and have a sense of humor doing it.

—**Criss Jami**

There is no returning to the past. There is no *new normal*. We are there. It is the *now normal*. Moving forward is our only option. Creativity and innovation must become part of that normal. Thinking *what if* is code for innovation. A key to innovation is to focus on a theme. For example, someone might focus on water, another person might focus on technology, yet another on communication. We don't have time or the energy to do everything. Only a few people, such as Leonardo da Vinci, could do that. Having a theme to focus on allows us to save our energy and time for what is most important to us.

Innovation is about creating something new. It doesn't necessarily mean replacing something. It's about new ideas. With your theme in mind, go out and start wondering, *What if?*

Look at Stuff in Plain Sight

Innovation develops as we go back to asking questions and challenging basic assumptions. Begin by examining ordinary objects, events, or processes that are in plain sight, right there in front of us. Consider their original purpose and history. What if they could be updated? What if something could be added or deleted? When people-watching, notice what people do every day. What if you could help them do it better or faster, or slower and more mindfully, or more efficiently. What if you could make it more fun? What do people complain about? What are they sick and tired of? What if you could fix it? What if you could find a new use for ordinary things? What if you could combine two ordinary things? What if you could make a complicated thing easy? Or mobile? Or self-service?

What ordinary things do we take for granted? What if we questioned any product or process that is more than five years old? For example, how we buy groceries has been basically the same for a century. My pet peeve is how we put groceries into the cart, put groceries on the counter to be scanned, put groceries back into the cart, take groceries out of cart into the car, and finally, take groceries out of car and into the house. This is the most time-wasting ritual I have ever had to endure. People, find a better way!

Grocery shopping has seen some change with the advent of prepared meal delivery, farmers markets, and produce boxes. With the beginning of the coronavirus pandemic in 2020, grocery shopping is starting to change more quickly. There is now curbside service, self-scan at check-out, and a variety of personal shopping, pickup, and home delivery services. (My husband and I now are blessed to have our groceries delivered.) Other ordinary things that have been around for more than five years include how we buy and sell houses and vehicles, how we save for retirement, and how we take vacations. All these areas have already started to change, with more change coming!

What if the ordinary thing ceased to exist? Physical banks are becoming fewer and farther between. A real bookstore is rare nowadays. What would be the human impact if the things we are used to disappeared? What would people need? The ordinary things in plain sight are exactly what people need, only perhaps updated or faster or more efficient.

Create a Prototype

It is not always necessary or financially feasible to jump in feet first, all or nothing. If you have an idea, consider testing the idea first. Start with small steps and learn from each step. Perhaps get a second opinion from someone you trust. If the idea is about a product, create a few samples and see how people respond to it. If the idea is about a process, test it for a short period of time and see what the outcome is. Restaurants often do this with new dishes. They create the new dish, offer it as a weekly special, and see how the dish is received. If received well, the dish makes it to the daily menu.

Creating a prototype simply means we are testing our idea before investing too much time or money into it. When I was a teenager, I got this idea to make green cakes with red frosting for Christmas. I could take orders and sell the cakes. I happily made my prototype, staying true to classic holiday colors with the cake bright evergreen-green and the frosting a dark true red. Sadly, the green cake turned out looking like algae or a green sponge, and the red frosting resembled something bloody. My sisters and mom wouldn't try even one bite. I tried a bite, but with my eyes closed. The family legend has it that even the dog wouldn't try it. The green and red Christmas cake, true to the holiday colors, was the ugliest cake in the world. I canceled that idea and moved on to gingerbread bears.

Create an Innovation Lab

An innovation lab is made up of a group of people who explore new ideas. They are sometimes called accelerators and incubators. Name it whatever you like. Some companies have large-scale innovation labs that can be part of the main company, or offshoots of it, according to wework.com. Those that aren't part of the company at all may be comprised of third parties. The scale of the innovation lab doesn't have to be large, and how it is implemented doesn't matter. It could be a group of like-minded friends or colleagues meeting in the basement. The only thing that matters is the innovation lab's purpose: dedicating time and energy to develop new ideas.

Curiously, a corporate innovation lab is traditionally bound by a set of rules. They have goals, metrics, budgets, and sometimes rules of behavior. If you want, develop your own rules. You might want to have a specific purpose, such as developing new services or replacing old products. One purpose for an innovation lab might be to explore what would disrupt or replace the status quo, or even make it disappear entirely.

How do you work and develop ideas in an innovation lab? Any way you want to! Reverse brainstorm. Think of new ideas and then find problems they can solve. Problem-solve with puzzles. Have parameters or criteria for problems, such as how to make toast without heat. Do research to find out what people need. Use critical thinking to analyze an existing product, system, service, or process. Develop ideas for prototypes. Use appreciative inquiry and dream big, then develop ideas to implement the dream.

Innovation is any way you find a way to do more for a client than anybody else does.

—Tony Robbins

Review: Think "What If"

Tools	Things to think about
Look at stuff in plain sight	Look around you. Identify three things that could use some updating, rethinking, or replacing.
Create a prototype	Consider an important task or project that you have. How could you test it, or part of it, by using a prototype?
Create an innovation lab	What group of people do you share ideas with?

Disrupt

I want to put a ding in the universe.

—Steve Jobs

Rock the boat. Make waves. Shake things up. Disrupt. To disrupt means to prevent something—a system, process, product, or event—from continuing as usual or as expected, often with the intent of creating something better. Some people call this positive disruption. Others call it reinvention. Lately, people have been referring to disruption as replacing whatever exists now with something totally new. I'm going to stick with rocking the boat and making waves, with the intent of making improvements.

Change Small Things

Disruption happens in the workplace and in our personal lives. My client, frazzled Jennifer, needed more quiet time after work when she got home. She was a chief operating officer and being groomed for a chief executive officer (CEO). She wanted only an hour to unwind at home. However, her children, husband, live-in mom, and dogs all expected her attention, which she gave to them exhaustedly and sometimes grumpily. She decided to start a new routine when she got home. She would take a bath. At first, this simple bath turned the house system into chaos. With time, the family adjusted as a new, reenergized Jennifer emerged from the tub.

Jennifer's little change in routine involved more than taking a bath. She needed a solution. Plus her solution needed to benefit her and her family. It needed to improve their world. This shows how disruption can be small yet have big effect. One day, Jennifer may need to change or delete her routine as her needs change. She will seek a new solution. This shows how disruption can be cyclic or emergent as new problems and new solutions appear.

Object

The Space Shuttle Challenger took off on January 28, 1986, with seven people on board. A little over one minute after it took off, it exploded.

It was later discovered that a failed O-ring seal caused the explosion. The engineers knew this was a possibility and had warned their leadership in advance, but it was decided the launch would proceed as planned. This is a tragic testament to the fact that sometimes we can object, and not be heard.

Nonetheless, we sometimes have a duty to object. There is always a risk that you won't be heard or taken seriously, or even that you'll be ostracized or punished. You may even lose your job because you spoke out against something. But, sometimes you have to object, be the whistleblower, and say, "That is not right."

How to object depends on the situation. If it involves a large organization, start by showing concern: "I am worried about the O-rings." Explain your concern: "The O-rings become brittle at low temperatures." Provide evidence or documentation: "Our tests show the O-rings will fail below a certain threshold. The temperature tonight will be below that threshold." Put your concern and objection in writing: "Here is my memo objecting to the launch and what the consequence might be if we do launch."

If our objection could possibly impact life or death, I feel we have a supreme duty to object. If nobody hears us, we need to put that objection into writing. Even if our objection doesn't concern a dire situation, I still feel we have a duty to say why we think something is wrong or not working. Explain the concern and rationale. Offer alternatives. If the boss doesn't listen to us, for self-protection, we still need to document the objection, maybe not in a formal memo, but in an e-mail or log entry or note on our calendar.

If our objection involves mistreatment of other people, in a perfect world, we need to object loudly enough for others to hear, be prepared to document the mistreatment, and report the mistreatment to leadership or the authorities. There are often consequences for this level of objection. Not everyone can risk getting fired or worse. If this is the case, seek safer ways to object.

Talk to Someone

When our objection involves mistreatment of people, or safety, moral, legal, or ethical issues, we may have a duty to object, and the only safe way to do this might be to tell someone in confidence. In some companies, we can talk to someone within the organization. These companies have procedures in place to report such things anonymously or confidentially through the human resources or equal opportunity channels. Some places have suggestion boxes or an ombudsman.

Talking to the media might work. A letter to the editor might work. We could request our name be withheld. We could also talk to a reporter. If we wanted to talk to the world, we could use social media or write a book under another name.

In severe cases, we could talk to the police.

Strike

The ultimate objection in the workplace is to stop work. Typically, strikes occur due to some type of grievance or organized purpose. A strike is intended to impact the organization to such a degree that the organization is forced to listen.

An official strike is usually organized through a union or other structured organization. A strike usually starts with negotiations, with people listing the changes or demands they want. A strike can involve a long period of time, and there are regulations and laws governing this. A strike is a serious situation. People may get fired or not paid. When coordinating the strike with a union, consider the potential impact on people as well as the reason for the strike.

Unofficial strikes are organized by groups and act as more of a protest. There may be picketing and speakers and sometimes blocking of access to a building or facility. The strike protest may or may not involve the employees of the organization. It may only involve protesters. Usually, these types of events are peaceful and last only a short period of time. Some become vulnerable to emotionalism and sometimes violence.

A single-person strike is another type of protest. The person may refuse to work, or stage something more dramatic, such as a hunger strike, or it could be a simple, singular act. A single-person strike protest is usually an objection to something and is organized by that person alone. Rosa Parks is one of the best examples of a single-person strike. In 1955, Rosa refused to give up her seat to a white passenger. This act may have been choreographed to challenge segregation laws, but the act itself was carried out by one woman who demonstrated incredible courage and a steadfast belief in equality.

Review: Disrupt

Tools	Things to think about
Change small things	What is one little change you could make in your life or workplace that would make it a better?
Object	Identify a time when you wanted to object to something but didn't. If you had a chance to do it over again, what might you do differently?
Talk to someone	If you saw something you felt was wrong in your workplace or neighborhood, what might you do?
Strike	What might cause you to consider participating in some form of strike?

Be Ready: The Universe Will Test You

Getting to the top has an unfortunate tendency to persuade people that the system is OK after all.

—Alain de Botton

One day, you will become the system. On that day, others will challenge you, object to what you do, or protest how you do it. Imagine the young spunky employee who has wild ideas, matures, becomes a CEO, and 20 years, later becomes the system. At that point, he or she may stop listening to new ideas or being innovative. It's easy to become entrenched and complacent, especially with time and especially with success. It is when we cease to be open to new ideas, to innovation, that we become stagnant, outdated, or worse yet, beholden or committed to a system that has become exploitative and uncaring.

When that day comes, when you become the system, keep rocking the boat. Take a moment and listen to a young, spunky employee with wild ideas.

Challenging the meaning of life is the truest expression of the state of being human.

—Viktor Frankl

CHAPTER 9

Save the World

We can no longer save the world by playing by the rules.

—Greta Thunberg

"I want to make an impact." "I want to create a movement." "I want to save the world." Along with happiness, these are the things my clients tell me when I ask them what they want in their job. Interestingly, I hear this from a wide spectrum of clients of all ages and cultures. Some clients are struggling to pay bills. Some clients are raising kids. Other clients say they are stuck in a meaningless job. They come to me for career coaching, in hopes of finding that happy job or a chance to save the world.

Save the World: What Does It Mean?

Neither to harm, nor be harmed.

—Epicurus (c. 350 BC)

Saving the world means doing one thing to make the world a better place. Just one thing. That thing can be little or big. It all counts. Just one thing. Jill wanted to save the world. She started crying when she told me how overwhelmed she felt. How each time she tried to save the world she saw 100 more things appear that needed saving. She could not grasp the concept of just one thing. She felt powerless, especially at work where she felt leadership and her coworkers didn't care. Regardless of what she did, the people in her workplace did not hear her rally cries.

However, they did hear her cries. Too *preachy* is how Jill's supervisor described her to me. Everything was a cause, the supervisor said. I worked with Jill for almost two years and helped her narrow in on the one cause that was closest to her heart. An area where she felt she could genuinely make a difference. Jill chose to focus her attention on dog rescue. She is now a certified foster dog mom and is learning how to rehabilitate and resocialize abused dogs. Jill is happier and her coworkers are more appreciative of her efforts. In fact, two of her coworkers have adopted foster dogs from her! Jill is saving the world. She is making positive impacts on the lives of other people and other creatures.

Here's a shout-out to my friend Leila, who adopted her cousin's babies, both born addicted to cocaine. The babies are now healthy, thriving teenagers. Leila broke the drug-and-poverty cycle for these two children. Leila is saving the world.

Both Jill and Leila are saving the world in fairly big ways. But remember, saving the world can be one little thing too. It can be turning off the faucet when we brush our teeth. It can be kindness to a stranger, learning about a new culture, picking up a piece of trash on the side of the road. Everything helps. We don't all have to be activists to save the world. However, we can all do little things that add up to making an appreciable and positive difference in our world.

Saving the world could also be doing something we consider ordinary or normal. For example, being a good parent. It seems obvious, ordinary, and parents generally don't see it as doing something to save the world, but it is. Well-loved and well-cared-for children grow up to be healthy, positive members of society. Another example of an ordinary activity that can help save the world is paying attention to our own personal health and wellness. Some of us pay attention to wellness, and some of us try and some of us don't. It doesn't seem like this would help save the world, but it does. When we are healthy, the world is better. We are happier, more resilient, and better able to contribute in a positive and meaningful way. We also might not tax the health care system so much if we practice preventive health care.

Saving the world is simply about doing our part, regardless how big or small or ordinary. It is also about doing it our way and being somewhat selective. We cannot take on all the challenges the world has to offer. That is overwhelming and creates the sense of powerlessness Jill felt. Yet, the magic is that we all have the power to save the world one piece at a time.

Save the World: Why?

People can save the world by the way they think and by the way they behave and what they hold to be important.

—Cyndi Lauper

The world is becoming smaller in a sense, more global. What we do in one part of the world impacts another part. There is no longer just *us*. Natural resources are limited. There are consequences to our behavior. We need to keep the Earth livable. There is inequity across the globe. Some people are starving, while others wallow in caviar. We need social justice. Why save the world? The answer will echo throughout this chapter: to make the world a better place.

Forgive

Forgiveness says you are given another chance to make a new beginning.
—Desmond Tutu

Consider this: The number one way to help save the world is to forgive the wrongs of the world. Why? Because humanity is not perfect. Our imperfection is part of the human condition. If we strive for perfection, we will never reach it. There are things in the world that seem perfect, like a sculpture by Donatello or Michelangelo. But I am sure those great artists found flaws in their work. It doesn't matter. Their work equals masterpiece, flaws, and all. We forgive the flaws in art. As humans, we are like flawed masterpieces. We need to forgive the flaws in us.

Webster's New World College Dictionary defines *forgiveness* as giving up resentment or the desire to punish; to stop being angry with; to pardon or to give up all claim to punish or exact penalty for (an offense); overlook.

Forgiveness seems to be present wherever there are humans. In Judaism, a person must go to those he has harmed to be entitled to forgiveness himself. A person must forgive to be Christian. Islam strongly encourages forgiveness. In Buddhism, forgiveness is seen as a practice to prevent harmful thoughts. In Hindu *dharma*, a person who does not forgive carries the baggage of harmful memories. *Ho'oponopono* is an ancient Hawaiian practice of reconciliation and forgiveness, combined with prayer, which uses the mantra: "I love you, I am sorry, please forgive me, thank you."

Forgive Others

Forgiveness does not mean we condone or ignore bad behavior. Forgiveness is about moving past the mistakes of others. It is about recognizing the humanity in others. Forgiveness has immense power. It can give others a second chance. It can do the same for us. It can break a bad cycle. It can help us heal old wounds or let go of emotions such as anger, resentment, or envy. It can help repair relationships. However, forgiving others is not always easy to do. It must be authentic. How do we forgive someone who has wronged us or hurt us? Sometimes, we need help.

> *There are imperfections in every human being, and you will always become unhappy if you look toward the people themselves. Therefore, do not look at the shortcomings of anybody; see with the sight of forgiveness.*
>
> **—Abdu'l-Baha**

A long time ago, I went to a counselor for help with interpersonal relationships. I came to understand I needed to forgive my biological father. I'd spent my entire adult life hating him, and it was showing up in my relationships. But, I could not forgive him. My counselor took me through a specific intervention designed to help me move past the bad memories of my father. I was finally able to realize that despite the abuse toward my mother, the drinking, and the aloofness, my biological father had done the best he could. He didn't know any better. It was a sad moment, and I suddenly felt sorry for him. I forgave him and was freed.

In the end, we must find our own way to offer forgiveness to others. Sometimes, we don't have to say a word. Other times, we must write something or have a conversation. Maybe it's a special meal, or a token, or simply a softened demeanor. In politics, it could be official amnesty. In banking, it could be loan forgiveness. In revolution, it could be reconciliation.

In the workplace, consider cultivating a forgiving culture. Allow people to make mistakes and learn from them. It will encourage innovation and risk-taking. If the term *forgiving* is too esoteric, give it another name.

People experience forgiveness differently, both the giving and receiving. We must determine our own definition of *forgiveness*. By creating a definition that fits us, we are more likely to forgive authentically. *Forgiveness takes time.* Be patient. It will not instantaneously occur. Forgiveness is a process not an event. We have to accept that people have wronged us, that it may not have been intentional, and realize that no one is keeping the wrong alive but ourselves.

Forgive Yourself

We have all done things we wish we had not. But, for some reason, it can be even harder to forgive ourselves. The situations are varied. It can be a simple situation where we made fools of ourselves or did a lousy job. Let's forgive ourselves, get up, brush the dust off, and move on. There are complex situations when we believe we did something wrong. Again, let's forgive ourselves, apologize, brush the dust off, and move on. If the other person doesn't forgive us, brush the dust off one more time and move on. And then, there are very serious situations that involve crime. Let's forgive ourselves again, apologize, ask for forgiveness, and pay for the consequences of our action. In most of these situations, forgiving ourselves allows us to move forward into a better world for ourselves, thus helping the world itself be a better place.

Sometimes, traumatic events can cause people to have feelings of guilt or self-hatred. This is especially true for the victims of trauma. Sometimes people who survive a crisis experience survivor's guilt. These people have done nothing wrong, but self-forgiveness can play a role in their recovery. If this is the situation you find yourself in and you are having a hard time forgiving yourself, please seek help. There are professionals out there who can assist you.

When a deep injury is done us, we never recover until we forgive.

—Alan Paton

Review: Forgive

Tools	Things to think about
Forgive others	Describe a time when someone forgave you.
Forgive yourself	What is the hardest part about forgiving yourself?

Re...

The idea is that each person does a small part—a "simple thing"—but understands that their part is just as essential as everyone else's.

—Javna

The prefix *re* means *again*, and it is an important element to saving the world. Our world is not limitless. We have limited resources. We have limits to what the world can withstand. Consider just one *re* to be part of your life.

Reuse

This *re* is about using it again. Consider how to use something again, regardless of how small or large the scale. If we can't reuse the item, perhaps we shouldn't buy it. Think about buying used clothing or items in thrift shops, flea markets, or yard sales. Think about purging your stuff and donating items so that others may use them.

Consider recycling. Many people do nowadays. Most plastic, glass, and paper goods can be recycled and used again to make a huge array of items, such as carpets, more paper, jewelry, or even kitchen cabinets. There are now recycling programs in most cities and towns all over the world. Perhaps composting works for you. This allows kitchen scraps to be reused to enhance garden soil. Check out the many ideas on YouTube for composting.

A controversial *re* is regifting. If you have been given a gift you don't like or can't use or already have three of, think about regifting. Don't let that gift go to waste. There is somebody out there who would like it.

Reduce

This *re* is about decreasing stuff. Consider how much we consume. Can it be reduced? It could be water, carbon-based energy, plastics, single-use items, or even food. Consider how much stress we have. Can that be reduced? How about how much money we spend? How about how much time we spend procrastinating? Is there one thing in our life that could bring us or the world added value if we reduced it?

Rethink

It may be time to reconsider things. For this *re*, it is about adjusting our mindset. My favorite example is how we must have perfect food. I've seen shoppers examine bananas for five minutes before selecting a perfect banana. Is that necessary? What about those single-use items so often made of paper and plastic? When I was on an island off the coast of Belize, I was amazed and horrified at the number of plastic products that were washed up on shore. Can we rethink how we use plastic products? My sister gave me a reusable straw last year. I keep it in my book bag.

What about rethinking how we think? In 2020, the year of the coronavirus pandemic, many of us had to rethink how we work, exercise, go to school, and stay connected. In this year of political unrest, many of us had to rethink how we vote. In this year of racial tension, many of us had to rethink what we believe and how we behave. This year, 2020, has been a time of intense rethinking. Our systems, values, and norms are all under scrutiny and being looked at with a new eye. All this, hopefully, will help make the world a better place.

Rescue

The rescue *re* is about delivering someone, some creature, or something from danger or difficulty. *Rescue* might also mean preserving a tradition, such as a language or art. Perhaps we are rescuing an old building or restoring a painting. Perhaps we are rescuing the planet, or most important, ourselves. Keep one life alive and save that world.

Refuse

This *re* simply means don't do it. Say no. Don't live your life according to others' demands or expectations unless you choose to do so. Refuse to be a victim. Refuse to allow evil or wrongdoing. Refuse to stop learning. Refuse to give up.

Review: Re...

Tools	Things to think about
Reuse	How can we reuse old souvenir t-shirts that we don't wear but that are sentimental and we don't want to get rid of them?
Reduce	What is one thing you'd like to reduce using?
Rethink	How do you feel about buying an ugly apple?
Rescue	What do you need rescuing from?
Refuse	Describe a time when you refused to do something.

Save Yourself

We're our own dragons as well as our own heroes, and we have to rescue ourselves from ourselves.

—Tom Robbins

Your very existence makes the world a better place. So, take care of you. A member of my Toastmasters group said it more elegantly. Nicole was giving an icebreaker speech, which involved introducing herself. She is a wellness coach and spoke about working with people who suffer from feelings of inferiority and insecurity. Her approach to helping her clients deal with and transcend these issues is to stress the truth that we are all worthy, that "we are enough."

We are enough because we are *intrinsically* worthy. Our very existence is proof of our value, our worthiness, and there is nothing we have to do to earn that. It is this *enoughness* or intrinsic value that allows us to have faith in ourselves. To honor our dreams and abilities, to answer the call to develop our skills, to continually improve, to follow our hearts. To create something that not only benefits our own lives, but the lives of the other worthy beings we are privileged to share this planet with.

Let Go of One Thing

We all, at one time or another, experience challenges, and sometimes find that the only way to get back to enjoying life is to let go of something. It could be as simple as a bad habit, a grudge, or some extra weight. Or, as complicated as an addiction, our home, or a relationship. It might be as painful as an old trauma or grief. Sometimes we need help to let go. Sometimes we discover that we simply can't let go and need to somehow learn to live with or manage our challenge or trauma or pattern of behavior.

Letting go is personal for each of us. We all have our dragons, big and small, simple and complex. Unless it is a friendly dragon, there is no reason to keep it around.

Find a Place in the World

Recognizing when you are happy and consciously cultivating that happiness is one of the ways to find our place in the world. If we are unhappy, investigate. Is it work? Is it health? Is it our environment? Is it where we're living? Consider working toward restoring a sense of joy. If our basic needs are being met, there's nothing more important.

For many of us, happiness and our sense of place in the world is to be found in our connections with others. There are so many ways to become connected to others, to find family, support, relationships, or like-minded coconspirators. Join a community, a meetup group, a spiritual center, a book club, a running club, or a neighborhood organization. Explore your ancestry.

I did a DNA test through 23andMe (a genomics and biotechnology company) and discovered that some of my long-ago ancestors were from Mongolia. Coincidentally (or not), I've always been fascinated by Mongolia. All of a sudden, I was connected to the planet in a different way. In addition to finding out more about my origins, I was matched with cousins I'd never known from my biological father's side of my family.

Find your place in this world by connecting with something out of this world. Stare at the stars. Every night my husband, Ken, and I take our dog out to pee, and we stare at the stars. There is very little artificial light to interfere with stargazing in rural New Mexico. Ken has an app on his phone that identifies constellations. We often see shooting stars, planets, satellites, and a couple of times, the space station. We stare up in wonder and feel how we are part of the whole magnificent, awe-inspiring multiverse, even if we are just tiny specks in space.

> *We are stardust brought to life, then empowered by the universe to figure itself out—and we have only just begun.*
> **—Neil deGrasse Tyson, *Astrophysics for People in a Hurry***

Practice Save-the-World Behaviors—Personal

Save-the-world behaviors are simple behaviors we can do in our personal lives. Just one of these behaviors can help make the world a better place.

Treat people with respect. We hear this all the time, to the point that it has become almost meaningless and trite. Perhaps we need to rethink this. Respect is a basic. Are we treating all people with respect and dignity, even if we disagree with them or don't like them? It's easy to be nice to someone who is nice.

One time, my husband and I hosted a homeowner's association meeting in our yard. It was a big picnic affair with a business meeting afterward. I tried to welcome everyone as they showed up. One couple, a lady and her husband, walked over to me and started complaining about all the homeowners and the association officers. The couple complained about the dues, road maintenance, and lights on people's front porches. They complained about too many people moving in, about barking dogs, and even about my husband (he was an officer). It was tough to stay polite.

"I see by the look on your face that you don't agree with me," the lady said. By now she was turning a bit red. She was ready for a fight.

"No, I don't agree with you, but I respect your opinion," I said without hesitation. I wanted to tell her, "Get off my lawn!" But, for a moment in time, I had good words and invited her to sit down and have something to eat. I saw her relax. Later, during the meeting, she complained some more and got other homeowners riled up. But, I was OK. I'd done my part.

Share. Do we share, whether it is food or fame? How about during the coronavirus? It's easy to share when we are sure of our own security and have plenty. It's not so easy when things become uncertain or scarce. When the coronavirus hit its first peak and shoppers were hoarding toilet paper and bleach, my neighbor, Kris, called and asked if we needed any toilet paper or cleaning supplies. Kris is saving the world.

Live happy. Do we engage in what makes us happy? This is easy, too, when it comes to our own happiness. How about other people? Do we honor what makes others happy?

Manage money. Do we manage money in a way that makes sense for us? I don't think money management is easy in any form. I had to learn it the hard way and have made my share of dumb money decisions. I've overspent, and at one time, didn't bother saving. It's hard for many of us. I am now trying to learn to be frugal. I can't emphasize enough how much money management can help save the world. It may be only your world, but it will give you security, a measure of independence, and freedom to make life's choices.

If you want to change the world, go home and love your family.

—Mother Teresa

Review: Save Yourself

Tools	Things to think about
Let go of one thing	What is one thing you don't want to do anymore?
Find a place in the world	What or who are you connected to? What or who do you wish to be connected with?
Save-the-world behaviors—personal	What makes you happy?

Save Your Business

The nation that leads in renewable energy will be the nation that leads the world 10, 20 years from now.

—James Cameron

Every business should consider doing something that's good for the world. For instance, on a huge scale, Amazon has set a goal to reduce their carbon emissions to net zero by 2040 and reach 100 percent renewable energy use by 2030. On a smaller scale, our local family restaurant provides a free turkey dinner with all the trimmings to anyone who walks into the restaurant on Thanksgiving Day.

Create Earth Goals

Think about establishing Earth goals that benefit and align with the mission of your company. A restaurant might set an Earth goal to reduce food waste, and a restaurant that's reducing food waste is going to save money. If we can create goals that also benefit our employees, even better, because there will then be a reason for each employee to support the mission. Provide incentives such as bonuses for supporting the Earth goal or promotions partially based on an employee's level of commitment to those goals.

Create People Goals

Consider including a people goal in your strategic plan, business model, or business operation. A people goal is anything pertaining to your business that influences, encourages, or helps people to reach out to other people. People goals help make business better.

There are traditional people goals, such as reducing turnover, improving new-employee orientations, and increasing professional development. There are also some more recent people goals that might involve child care arrangements, dogs in the workplace, flexible working hours, working from home, and wellness. Global people goals might involve partnering or collaborating or just communicating with another business in another part of the world. This might involve sharing cultures, sponsoring an intern from another country, becoming a digital pen pal with other people in the world, or meeting suppliers from other countries. All these initiatives help save the world by promoting education, inclusion, and partnering.

A business must be diverse for the sake of human dignity, but it must also be diverse to succeed into the future. Here's the bottom line, which is basically the line that shows the profits: If your business doesn't have a diverse workplace, your business is not going to succeed. Business has become too global to exclude people who don't look, behave, and think like us. That is dinosaur thinking. People are moving around the world. Businesses go to one place to make widget A and another place to make widget B. If businesses want to thrive, they must keep embracing the globalness of the world.

A traditional diversity goal for an organization typically involves an introduction-to-diversity class during a new-employee orientation, an annual mandatory one-hour class, and an official statement about diverse hiring practices. Note that there is no mention of people in this type of people goal. Consider this: Find the youngest or newest or most different employee in the organization. It doesn't matter how big or small the business. Have that person suggest a people goal for diversity.

Practice Save-the-World Behaviors—Professional

Practice save-the-world behaviors in the workplace. Just like the personal save-the-world behaviors, implementing just one of these behaviors can make a difference.

Consider the human impact of change. When a product or business model or procedure needs to change, there will be a human impact. It is not about publishing the policy change and expecting people to happily comply. We need to understand how those changes might impact employees.

My client Robert had worked at his company for 17 years. He loved his job, was outspoken about it, and proud of the legacy he would leave the company whenever he retired, though he had no desire to retire. The day came when Robert's management upgraded or replaced all the "old, obsolete, inefficient, and inaccurate" systems, the systems Robert had created. Suddenly Robert felt old, obsolete, inefficient, and inaccurate. Unneeded. When he showed hesitation or lack of enthusiasm or, worse, objected, he was reprimanded for not being a team player. If you were the leader of this organization, how would you implement a major change, how would you deal with the Roberts? My only suggestion for managing change is to consider the impact on people.

In the end, Robert felt so demoralized and *thrown away* that no amount of leadership intervention could change things for him. He came to me for career coaching, not to enhance his current job, but to change careers. His goals were to retire early and start a second career.

Do not tolerate the bullies. Probably every business has bullies. I've personally seen bullying in law enforcement, health care, restaurants, and government organizations. I've heard of bullies in almost every other type of business. Bullying can take many forms: harassment, discrimination, hazing of new employees, intimidation, jokes, humiliation, or threats. Based on my experience, a workplace bully rides the fence of civility, knowing what the regulations allow or don't allow, knowing how to use language to insinuate and incite, and knowing how to slink into the shadows if threatened. Bullies like to prey on those they perceive as weak or vulnerable.

Carole was continually approached and harassed by Alan, the assistant manager at the chain restaurant where she worked. Carole is quiet, an introvert, and tends to shy away from crowds and overstimulating places. She presents as weak and vulnerable to a bully. Every day Alan insulted and taunted Carole, making suggestive remarks that embarrassed and humiliated her. When Carole reported Alan to the manager, the manager said Carole was overreacting. At this point, the manager had a wonderful opportunity to help save the world, but he didn't grab it. Instead, Alan continued to bully Carole, and she decided to secretly look for another job and figure out how to change her image. That's when I met Carole.

Six months later, Carole was hired to be a sous chef in a nice restaurant. When she interviewed for the job, she had a list of questions to ask the interviewer, including "What is your philosophy about food?" and "What is your policy about workplace bullying?"

Take care of new people. It's never easy to be the new person on the block. I believe in mentoring and onboarding new employees. Today's employees are not staying 20 years in one place anymore. This is all the more reason to onboard them, mentor them, and give them a reason to stay. If we do this, even if they don't stay after three to five years, we're still going to have three to five years of good service.

Cultivate an abundance mindset. There is enough for everyone. Abundance is about generosity and service and giving as well as being open to receiving what we're worth. It's also about imagining the future world. What kind of world do you want to live in? The abundance mindset says we want to live in a world where there is enough for everyone.

Review: Save Your Business

Tools	Things to think about
Create Earth goals	What could you do to support the Earth in your workplace?
Create people goals	What kind of people goals might be appropriate for your workplace?
Practice save-the-world behaviors—professional	Describe a time when you were traumatized by a big change in your workplace. If you had been in charge, how would you have managed that change?

Practice Gratitude

Gratitude is not a limited resource, nor is it costly. It is abundant as air. We breathe it in but forget to exhale.

—Marshall Goldsmith

Yes, I know. Gratitude is an odd way to save the world. However odd, gratitude makes the world a better place in some inexplicable way. At its simplest, gratitude is expressing appreciation. It is a gesture of thankfulness. At its most complex, gratitude changes our awareness of the world. Gratitude makes our world bigger.

My sister Laura took care of my mom during my mom's last two years. Toward the end, Laura was exhausted. She had taken no time for herself, and she was worn out, resentful, and grumpy. Laura sent me a text, telling me how angry and fed up she was. She wanted to move our mom out of her house; she wanted her life back. However, my mom did not want to move. Taking care of my mom drained Laura of all her energy.

"Laura, have courage and strength," I replied. "Mother has very little time left. Focus on what you are grateful for."

An hour later, Laura sent me a text: "Oh my God, I'm so stupid... Thank you for reminding me... I really am grateful she is with me! I'm going to make her a special supper with one perfect fresh strawberry for dessert." I don't know if Laura was telling me what I wanted to hear, but her words felt sincere to me. She followed-through, made supper and remained gentle with my mom. Through gratitude, Laura was able to see beyond her own pain, beyond the world she was experiencing in that moment of frustration. Her world got bigger. My mom died a few days later. Thank you Laura.

Practice Gratitude Daily

Gratitude does something to our brain. It creates positive feelings and a deeper connection or awareness of the world. There is also research that suggests gratitude can impact our health in a good way by reducing feelings of stress and lowering blood pressure.

My husband and I practice gratitude every night. We are not allowed to say we are grateful for each other, our family, our little dog, or God. Those are implicit.

"What are you grateful for?" Ken asks as we look at the stars during our evening take-the-little-dog-out-to-pee ritual.

I'm tired from staring at my computer all day and all I want is to get back inside and watch my Chinese costume drama on TV. Sighing, I reply, "Getting a 95 on my paper, staying within my calories, and exercising."

"What else?" Ken asks.

"Let's see," I say. I struggle and search. "I am grateful for your help with my paper. I am sure your feedback got me the good grade. I know I've said it a million times, but I'm grateful for the chance to go back to school."

I'm not so tired anymore. I feel proud that I'm in school and doing well. Ken points out Mars, and then turns and points out Jupiter and Venus. The Milky Way is a swath of blurred stars over our house. Where is Proxima Centauri, I wonder. Could we live there?

"What are you grateful for?" I ask Ken.

A daily practice of gratitude will save the world little by little, day by day. A partner to practice it with makes it special, but a partner isn't necessary. It could be a solitary activity and be just as beautiful and gratifying. The more we practice gratitude, the more it changes us. But, we can still do it *our way*.

Start a Gratitude Journal

The quiet of writing without an audience may be more comfortable for expressing gratitude. And, it doesn't have to be writing. It could be drawing or doodling or list-making.

Post on Social Media

This is a digital form of a gratitude journal. I had a client who, in preparation for heart surgery, decided to write a personal gratitude post every single day on Facebook. After her successful surgery, she kept it up for an entire year. She had to dig deep to find something new to feel grateful for every single day. She shared that this daily exercise helped her go through the surgery and recover from it, because staying in the energy of gratitude bolstered her mood and reminded her of why she was alive and why she wanted to stay alive. The posts also brought her a lot of positive support from her family and friends. That is the magic of gratitude.

Choose any social media you want and post any number of times you want. Words, photos, videos, memes, or music. It all works.

Find a Gratitude Rock

It doesn't have to be a rock. It's more like a token or a charm or some little thing that reminds you to be thankful. Some people use a smooth rock, like a worry stone. They carry the rock in their pocket or purse all the time. Whenever they touch the rock or hold it, they recall the good things in life. I collect regular old ordinary rocks and put them in my garden or around the house. I especially like rocks from rocks from beaches: from Homer, Alaska; Andros Island, the Bahamas; the Gold Coast in Spain— everywhere I meet a beach. I also have rocks from friends who traveled places. Each time I see the rocks, I remember the beach or friend and am grateful for knowing them.

A friend uses shells instead of rocks. Each shell is something she is grateful for. Her favorite shell is a giant oyster shell from the Puget Sound that her husband gave her on their first anniversary. Some people specialize in a certain color of rocks or write on the rocks or paint the rocks. I have a little rock painted to look like a rabbit.

Other people make a rock cairn, a stack of rocks that signifies you've reached a certain landmark, especially the top of the mountain. I made many cairns growing up, hiking the hillsides of the Denali tundra. I plan to put cairns in my garden made of smooth round stones, a cairn for each major accomplishment and major event. When I see them as I walk around, I can remember and say thank you.

It's not important how we express gratitude. It is only important that we do.

The essence of all beautiful art, all great art, is gratitude.
—Friedrich Nietzsche

Review: Practice Gratitude

Tools	Things to think about
Practice gratitude daily	What are you grateful for today?
Start a gratitude journal	If you wanted to create a gratitude journal, how would you do it?
Post on social media	What do you like best about social media?
Find a gratitude rock	How would you use a rock or some other item to remind you to be grateful for something?

Be Ready: The Universe Will Test You

What, am I supposed to run around in a little red cape and save the world?

—Kyle Chandler

We stand ready, arms akimbo. We have our superhero cape and lean into the wrongs of the world ready to fight to save the world. Yet we must tread carefully. Our passion to save the world can sometimes backfire or be misplaced or even turn to violence. We must remember that no matter how noble our cause, it is not for us to dictate to others how to live their lives.

I coached Carlos for three years. He lives in a tiny, remote town with his parents, two dogs, a cat, and some chickens. When I met him, he was an unemployed journeyman electrician. He was barely paying his bills with government assistance. The government hired me to help him find a job. He presented with a lack of confidence and minimal social skills. He also had no computer skills and struggled with self-direction. Yet, he'd gone to school and passed the exam to become a journeyman electrician! I was determined to save Carlos.

I confirmed his journeyman electrician skills and taught him how to interview, shake hands, and write resumes. I referred over 100 jobs to him. Nothing. I kept pushing. If I could help him land a journeyman electrician job, I could change his world. However, there were no journeyman electrician jobs near where he lives, and he refused to consider jobs that required him to travel. He needed to stay near the family farm and look after his elderly parents. I pushed more and suggested that he start his own mobile electrician business with just a van for his equipment. He liked that idea but has yet to get that business off the ground.

I had searched for how to support and guide Carlos with no success. I finally asked my mentor coach for help. She asked me to describe Carlos and the world of Carlos.

I told her that Carlos feels a strong filial duty to his parents, much stronger than his calling to work as a journeyman electrician. His voice becomes animated and his eyes light up when he talks of his duty to his parents. "Who else would take care of them?" If he were not there, his parents might be neglected or put in a facility. "We are comfortable and have what we need." He regards his journeyman's certificate with intense pride, but his duty to his parents comes first.

"What do you see?" my mentor coach asked me. I saw it clearly.

"Carlos doesn't need saving," I said. "He is already saving the world."

Epilogue

I wrote this book in the midst of the coronavirus pandemic of 2020. At the beginning of the pandemic, I decided I didn't want this year to be about hiding or capitulating to fear. I wanted to accomplish something that was meaningful for me personally.

I'm not famous. I'm not a billionaire. I've made plenty of mistakes. I'm not special, but I'm a happy person. I like my life and wouldn't have it any other way. Above all, I value life and pray that people don't waste their lives muddling along, doing things they don't want to do or that don't make them happy.

One of the ways I've chosen to save the world is to become a career coach and help people create meaningful lives. Writing this book brought a sense of purpose to my life, and I hope it inspires you to reach for your dreams and find what makes you happy to be alive.

This was my story.... One day Denali will call me. Denali has no rules. Sometimes she allows climbers to reach the top. Mostly when Denali finishes with you, nothing remains except your remains frozen in those icy layers. You, too, may cry or pray for answers, but Denali will ignore you. Or so you think. But she is always there to remind us that there are no answers, only this ice-crystal sword we live under. Only this warning: This is your life. Do not waste it.

—Gail Summers, *Across the Inlet*

About the Author

As a career coach, **Gail Summers** tries to help clients build successful careers, based on their definition of success. Instead of retiring, Summers has gone back to school to pursue PhD in Industrial Psychology with a research focus on happiness in the workplace. When not trying to save the world, she is out digging in the dirt of her massive outlier rock garden.

Index

OTHER TITLES IN THE BUSINESS CAREER DEVELOPMENT COLLECTION

Vilma Barr, Consultant, Editor

- *Fast Forward Your Career* by Simonetta Lureti and Lucio Furlani
- *Emotional Intelligence at Work* by Richard M. Contino and Penelope J. Holt
- *Negotiate Your Way to Success* by Kasia Jagodzinska
- *How to Make Good Business Decisions* by J.C. Baker
- *Ask the Right Questions; Get the Right Job* by Edward Barr
- *Personal and Career Development* by Claudio A. Rivera and Elza Priede
- *Your GPS to Employment Success* by Beverly A. Williams
- *100 Skills of the Successful Sales Professional* by Alex Dripchak
- *Getting It Right When It Matters Most* by Tony Gambill and Scott Carbonara
- *The Power of Belonging* by Sunita Sehmi
- *The Champion Edge* by Alan R. Zimmerman
- *Shaping Your Future* by Rita Rocker-Craft
- *Finding Your Career Niche* by Anne S. Klein

Concise and Applied Business Books

The Collection listed above is one of 30 business subject collections that Business Expert Press has grown to make BEP a premiere publisher of print and digital books. Our concise and applied books arc for…

- Professionals and Practitioners
- Faculty who adopt our books for courses
- Librarians who know that BEP's Digital Libraries are a unique way to offer students ebooks to download, not restricted with any digital rights management
- Executive Training Course Leaders
- Business Seminar Organizers

Business Expert Press books are for anyone who needs to dig deeper on business ideas, goals, and solutions to everyday problems. Whether one print book, one ebook, or buying a digital library of 110 ebooks, we remain the affordable and smart way to be business smart. For more information, please visit www.businessexpertpress.com, or contact sales@businessexpertpress.com.

Lightning Source UK Ltd.
Milton Keynes UK
UKHW022038161221
395720UK00009B/437